Heiko Hoffmann

Unsupervised Learning of Visuomotor Associations

Logos Verlag Berlin

λογος

Bibliografische Information Der Deutschen Bibliothek

Die Deutsche Bibliothek verzeichnet diese Publikation in der Deutschen
Nationalbibliografie; detaillierte bibliografische Daten sind im Internet über
http://dnb.ddb.de abrufbar.

Dissertation, Universität Bielefeld, Technische Fakultät

ISBN 3-8325-0858-9

Logos Verlag Berlin
Comeniushof, Gubener Str. 47,
10243 Berlin
Tel.: +49 030 42 85 10 90
Fax: +49 030 42 85 10 92
INTERNET: http://www.logos-verlag.de

to my parents, mother-in-law,

Su-Chen, and Richard

Acknowledgments

First, I like to thank my supervisor Ralf Möller. He provided many of the basic ideas, gave support, and was always ready with help. Ralf took lots of care that things worked out smoothly. Furthermore, I appreciate the freedom given by him during this research. Holk Cruse kindly accepted to review this thesis; and Helge Ritter and Jannik Fritsch readily joined my thesis committee.

In the first two years of my PhD work, I shared an office with Wolfram Schenck. This sharing was a very pleasant experience. Wolfram gave valuable contributions to this thesis: I used his implementation of the multi-layer perceptron network and his implementation of the inverse kinematics for the robot arm; to control this arm, he also provided a C++ library; in addition, he took the photos in figure 6.3 and provided comments on chapters 1 and 8.

To set up the robots and to get them running, I received help from Bruno Lara, Janos Kovats, Helmut Radrich, Rainer Giedat, Fiorello Banci, and Karl-Heinz Honsberg. Henryk Milewski provided a computer model of the robot arm. Moreover, he and DaeEun Kim fed me with stimulating lunchtime discussions. During my visits at Bielefeld University, I was kindly assisted by Angelika Deister, particularly in organizing my PhD defense.

I thank my parents for all their help, which in the first place gave me the opportunity to pursue a PhD, my mother-in-law, who traveled the long way from Taiwan to Germany to help us, my wife Su-Chen for her endless support and love, and my son Richard for his patience (for waiting with his birth until the day after my PhD defense). To them, I dedicate this book.

This work was supported by the Max Planck Institute for Human Cognitive and Brain Sciences in Munich.

Contents

Chapter 1

Introduction

1.1 Motivation

Perception, according to the ninth definition from the Oxford English Dictionary (Simpson and Weiner, 1989), refers to the "the neurophysiological processes, including memory, by which an organism becomes aware of and interprets external stimuli or sensations." For Tolman (1932), perception is any expectation of an external object or situation "when this expectation results primarily from present stimuli" (p. 452).

It is still unclear how neural processes lead to an interpretation of external stimuli, and how 'seeing' comes about. At least, we know that most of seeing needs to be learned[1] (see Gregory (1998) for a review). For example, humans that grow up blind and gain vision as an adult have difficulties to make sense of their visual experience.

To learn to interpret visual experience, active movement is important. Kittens that are only *passively* moved, while observing their environment, show impaired visual-guided movements (Held and Hein, 1963). In humans, the influence of action[2] on perceptual learning can be seen in visual adaptation studies, visual recognition studies, and fMRI experiments (section 1.4.2). This link between action and perception is also plausible from an evolutionary perspective. Our survival depends on our interaction with the world, and therefore, the potential to see something that is irrelevant to our behavior will disappear through natural selection.

In this thesis, visual perception is explored from the perspective of sensorimotor models, for example, models providing a mapping from sensory data to motor commands, or inversely from motor commands to sensory data. For example, according to this concept, the shape of an object is understood

---

[1]Among these qualities are the perception of three-dimensional space and distance; on the other hand, motion detection seems to be genetically preprogrammed (Gregory, 2003).

[2]In this thesis, 'action' refers to active movement.

1

('perceived') by associating appropriate grasping postures. Such a sensorimotor approach is an alternative to a pure sensory image analysis that extracts labels such as 'triangular' or 'elongated'. In this thesis, robots are used to test this sensorimotor approach to perception.

To acquire sensorimotor models, infants spend years to learn the effects of their actions. They can do this without a teacher, by initially moving their limbs (seemingly) randomly. Also the robots used in this work collect training data by exploring the sensory effects of their random motor commands. Then, machine learning techniques make sense out of the sensorimotor data by finding simplified representations. Thus, relations within the data are learned in an 'unsupervised' way. This thesis tackles problems that arise in the learning of sensorimotor models, for example, ambiguities and generalization.

1.2   Outline and contributions

This thesis introduces unsupervised learning algorithms for arbitrary sensorimotor associations. The experimental and mathematical understanding of these algorithms will be given considerable space. Two robot setups—a robot arm and a mobile robot—serve as a test bed for our sensorimotor theory of perception of space and shape, specifically for the learning and application of visuomotor models.

The remainder of the **Introduction** focuses on two points: the background of the sensorimotor approach to perception and the description of existing learning techniques. The first point covers experiments that show an influence of action on perception and reviews hypothesis on perception based on sensorimotor models. The second point covers artificial neural networks and their application to sensorimotor models. These networks comprise feedforward networks, recurrent networks, and Kohonen's self-organizing maps (Kohonen, 1995).

Chapter 2 reviews existing methods related to the new unsupervised learning techniques. The collection of the sensorimotor data is a distribution of data points in some high-dimensional space. The goal of learning is to find an approximation of this distribution. Two strategies are used: first, fitting a mixture of ellipsoids to the data, and second, mapping the data to a higher-dimensional space in which they can be approximated by a single hyper-plane. The first uses a combination of vector quantization and principal component analysis (PCA). Here, PCA is restricted to a region within the distribution; hence, it is called local PCA. A mixture of local PCA relates to a probability density model of the data (Bishop, 1995). The second strategy is based on a non-linear extension of PCA that is called kernel PCA (Schölkopf et al., 1998b).

Chapter 3 describes new algorithms to determine the parameters of a mixture of local PCA from a data distribution. One algorithm combines the vector quantizer Neural Gas (Martinetz et al., 1993) with local PCA. Another algorithm extends the mixture of probabilistic PCA (Tipping and Bishop, 1999), such that it can cope with sparse distributions, like typical sensorimotor data. Both algorithms are tested on synthetic data and on the classification of hand-written digits.

Chapter 4 describes a novel pattern-association method that builds on the mixture of local PCA from chapter 3. Input and output are parts of a data point in the sensorimotor space. In this space, the input portion of a data point is the offset from zero of a constrained subspace. The intersection of this subspace with the mixture of ellipsoids gives a completed data point, which yields the output portion in its components. The method resembles a recurrent neural network, since input and output components can be chosen *after* learning, and arbitrary distributions can be approximated instead of just functions. The new method learns to complete images and learns the kinematics of a simulated robot arm with redundant degrees of freedom. The latter task demonstrates the advantage over feed-forward networks. In addition, the dependence on the number of input dimensions will be analyzed experimentally and theoretically.

Chapter 5 introduces an alternative pattern-association method, which is based on kernel PCA. A subspace spanned by the principal components of the distribution's mapping into an infinite-dimensional space serves as a representation of the data. Here, recall is a descent in a potential field, and its region of attraction is the principal subspace. With the help of a kernel function, all computation can be done in the original space. The new pattern-association method is tested on synthetic data and on the kinematic arm model from chapter 4.

In **chapter 6**, the pattern-association methods from chapter 4 and 5 are applied to a visuomotor model for a robot arm. The robot is equipped with a two-finger gripper and a camera. The task of the robot is to grasp an object by associating an image of the object with an arm posture. Image processing is necessary and mimics biological functions. Furthermore, it proved to be of advantage to use a population coding for the joint angles, the object's position, and its orientation within the image. The experiment shows that the robot can perceive an object's position and orientation in space by simulating an arm posture suitable to grasp the object.

Chapter 7 presents a forward model for a mobile robot with an omni-directional camera. The model predicts the sensory consequence of a motor command. By anticipating the effect of a sequence of motor commands, the robot can either select actions that lead to defined goal states or use the simulation of actions to estimate its location in space and its distance to obstacles. In learning the sensorimotor model, a multi-layer perceptron proved to be better than the newly developed pattern-association described in chapter 4. The reason for this difference is explored.

Chapter 8 sums up the results and puts them into relation with each other. **Appendix A** describes some common statistical tools. Some of the algorithms used are presented in **Appendix B**. Mathematical proofs can be found in **Appendix C**. **Appendix D** shows samples from a database of hand-written digits, and **Appendix E** contains lists with notations, symbols, and abbreviations.

Chapter 3 to 7, further appendix B.3 and appendix C contain the contributions of this work. Parts of this research has been published beforehand. These parts are:

Section 3.2.1 and 3.4:   the extension of Neural Gas to local PCA and its application to digit classification (Möller and Hoffmann, 2004).

Section 4.2 and 4.5:   the pattern recall based on a mixture model and its application to a kinematic arm model (Hoffmann and Möller, 2003).

Section 6.2.2 and 6.2.3: some of the methods for the robot-arm experiments: the data collection (slightly different version) and the image processing that extracts the orientation of an object (Schenck et al., 2003).

Chapter 7:   the anticipation based on a multi-layer perceptron, the goal-directed movements, and the estimate of the robot's location (Hoffmann and Möller, 2004).

Appendix C.3:   the theoretical prediction of the error accumulation for the anticipation task in chapter 7 (Hoffmann and Möller, 2004).

1.3   Why using robot models?

'What I cannot create, I do not understand.'

R. P. Feynman[3]

Understanding the brain requires more than knowing which brain part processes which function. Understanding must include *how* specific tasks are

---

[3]This sentence was written on his blackboard, see S. W. Hawking (2001), *Das Universum in der Nußschale*, p. 91.

solved. Without a hypothesis on the function of a neural structure, anatomical and electro-physiological data are often difficult to interpret. Thus, models of the brain function are developed. Although certain details of the model can be tested by experiment (for example, whether, in a certain cortex region, an object's position is coded in eye-centered coordinates (Batista et al., 1999)), the overall working of the model usually relies on human intuition, which could be wrong. Therefore, a good test seems to be to construct a system able to do the task studied. This construction is 'synthetic modeling', which may be understood as an extension to its analytical counterpart.

In synthetic modeling, robots have an advantage over simulations because the latter are more likely to oversimplify a problem (Brooks, 1986a). To be feasible, simulations will usually include only those parts that seem essential from the perspective of the scientist. Thus, in a robot setup, problems may emerge that have not been foreseen in a simulation. For example, different from most simulations, in the real world, the sensory input is noisy, and this noise may make a model break down.

It remains arguable how good a robot can model biology (see Webb (2001) and the open peer commentaries following that article). The solution found by a robotics engineer might be different from the one realized in the brain (the neural circuits differ from the engineered ones). Nevertheless, being forced to solve a problem in the real world results at least in an understanding of the difficulties that need to be overcome. Therefore, testing models on robots helps to develop an intuitive understanding of brain function.

1.4 The sensorimotor approach

This section starts with a discussion on the limitations of the 'symbol systems' perspective to perception. The symbolic approach, pursued traditionally by artificial intelligence, assumes a one-way processing of visual information from raw sensory data to symbolic representations. The sensorimotor approach, in contrast, assumes that visual perception depends on a motor representation. This section reviews experimental evidence of an (involuntary and subconscious) influence of action on the visual perception, and closes with a collection of hypothesis on perception based on sensorimotor models.

1.4.1 Limitations of symbolic representations

According to the symbol-systems approach, every item in the world is mapped onto a symbol. For example, the image of a chair is mapped onto the label 'chair'. After having labeled all items, every subsequent task is solved by manipulating the labels. For example, the 'chair' is in the 'middle' of the room, I am standing at the '*door*'. Therefore, given the known geometry of the room, I need to '*go forward*' before I can '*sit down*'.

This strategy has been followed by the so-called 'Good Old Fashioned Artificial Intelligence' or short GOFAI (Haugeland, 1986). GOFAI was successful to cope with tasks that are difficult for humans, like playing chess, but GOFAI did not succeed on tasks that humans do effortlessly, like reaching for a pen on a cluttered desk. This difficulty suggests that the brain has a different strategy for solving these tasks (Pfeifer and Scheier, 1999). Moreover, following the symbolic approach, the mappings from real objects onto symbols were usually done by a human, leaving only the symbol manipulation to the machine. Therefore, the approach distracts from the real problem of object manipulation (Brooks, 1986b). As it turned out, this gap to the real world could never be closed (Pfeifer and Scheier, 1999).

1.4.2 Experimental evidence

While artificial intelligence and robotics only started recently to recognize the influence of action on the visual perception, experimental psychology studied this influence for more than a century. An *active* movement (or manipulation) that causes a sensory change will alter the corresponding perception in a following passive observation condition. Furthermore, experiments show that neurons exist that fire both during active movement and perception.

Visual adaptation

Several studies show that adaptation to visual distortion depends on activity. I start with an old but illustrative study, and then present newer evidence. To find an answer to the question why we see the world upright despite retinal inversion, Stratton (1896, 1897) did experiments with goggles that revolve sight by 180°. In the main experiment (Stratton, 1897), he wore the goggles over a period of eight days. In the beginning, everything looked upside down and the eye-hand coordination was strongly handicapped (manual operations were easier if done blindly). At the end (the last two days), the conflict between the operation of the hands and the visual impression vanished. Stratton could even have the impression that everything looked the right way up. For him, a new representation was learned next to the old one. In general, active operations enhanced the switch to the new representation; he notes, "In rapid, complicated, yet practiced movements, the harmony of the localization by sight and that by touch or motor perception—the actual identity of the positions reported in these various ways—came out with much greater force than when I sat down and passively observed the scene" (p. 356). His findings therefore suggest that the interaction with the world leads to our impression of upright vision. From a study with monkeys that wore inverting goggles for months, Sugita (1996) reported a reorganization of the visual cortex. But, the effect of the adaptation on perception is still debated, and some see Stratton's description of the inversion of vision as exaggerated (Linden et al., 1999).

The importance of active movement in visual adaptation has been further observed in experiments with wedge-prism goggles and with underwater vision. Wedge-prism goggles displace sight by a couple of degrees to one side. In the experiment by Held and Freedman (1963), subjects reached to target points either actively or passively (external force), while wearing these goggles. After the removal of the goggles, the subjects showed after-effects, resulting from an adaptation to the changed visual projection, only in trials following active movements. In the same direction goes a study with divers (Luria and Kinney, 1970). When wearing diving goggles under water, objects appear closer to the untrained eye; this also leads to pointing errors. Here, adaptation was faster if the divers were engaged in activities like placing a weight on a checkerboard grid.

Given these two studies, it may be still argued that the adaption is on a low sensorimotor level, and that it does not influence perception. However, a study with left-hemispatial-neglect patients (which have a neurological deficit of attention, perception, and doing actions within their left-sided space) shows that prism adaptation also involves higher-level space perception (Rossetti et al., 1998). After doing pointing tasks with prisms, the patients—after removal of the goggles—could turn their awareness toward the neglected side (to a degree corresponding to the visual shift resulting from the prism). This awareness shift was demonstrated with tests on reading and on drawing. A following study could induce neglect in healthy humans (Colent et al., 2000). The adaptation to left-deviating prisms resulted in a rightward bias for perceptual and motor line-bisection tasks.

Also a treadmill (a conveyor-belt for indoor exercises) can alter your perception. After being exposed to a static visual input while running, a runner observes an after-effect when standing still. The surroundings appear (erroneously) to be moving toward the runner (Pelah and Barlow, 1996). If our interpretation of vision would depend solely on the retinal image, such a finding could not be explained.

Recognition tasks

Active control has further a positive effect on recognition tasks. Simons and Wang (1998) compared active to passive viewpoint changes. Familiar objects (like a brush or a mug) were presented on a circular table. Subjects had to remember the position of all objects. Two set of trials were compared. In the first set, the subjects walked to another viewing position, and in the second set, they were either passively moved (in a wheelchair) or the table was rotated (the change of the retinal image was the same in all conditions). In the active condition, changes were recognized easier. In a different study, novel 3D objects were presented on a computer screen (Harman et al., 1999). In the training block, subjects could either explore the objects by rotating them with a trackball, or they passively observed the rotated objects. Later, in the test block, actively explored objects could be easier recognized than passively observed ones (in an 'old/new' discrimination task). The advantage of active exploration over passive observation was further found in virtual reality studies (James et al., 2002).

Neuroscience

The action-perception link has also a physiological basis. In the macaque monkey, neurons have been found that fire both during the grasping of objects and during the observation of graspable objects (Rizzolatti et al., 1988; Murata et al., 1997; Rizzolatti and Fadiga, 1998). These neurons have been termed 'canonical F5 neurons' (located in the premotor cortex, area F5)[4]. They are specific to the type of goal, for example, to precision grips or power grips, and also to the size of observed objects (which require different grip types). Furthermore, they do not respond to objects out of reach.

This link between action and perception is not only restricted to the direction from vision to premotor neurons; actions can also influence the activation of the visual cortex. On humans, using functional magnetic resonance imaging (a tool to visualize the local energy consumption in the vital brain), Astafiev et al. (2004) could show that the area in the visual cortex that responds to observing body parts of other humans is also active during goal-directed movements of the observer's own limbs.

Conclusion

Many experiments have shown that one's own actions influence perception, especially perceptual learning. Active movements (as opposed to passive ones) yield an easier adaptation to visual distortion and yield a better performance in recognition tasks. Moreover, neural responses that represent both action and perception suggest a direct association between the two.

---

[4]In recent years, the 'mirror neurons' became more popular (Rizzolatti et al., 2001). These neurons also fire when the monkey sees the grasping movement done by someone else. They have been therefore linked to imitation. However, this thesis does not deal with imitation.

Thus, at least some forms of visual perception seem to be based on learning visuomotor associations[5].

1.4.3 Perception based on sensorimotor models

This section reviews different hypotheses on the functional principles of perception. All relate to action, and present an alternative to the classical perspective of a one-way processing from sensors to motor actuators.

Affordances

According to Gibson (1977), an object directly offers its behavioral meaning to the observer. This is called 'affordance'. Gibson (1977) defined that "the affordance of anything is a specific combination of the properties of its substance and its surfaces taken with reference to an animal" (p. 67). Thus, affordances are, for example, a rigid surface affording support ('step-on-able'), or a chair being 'sit-on-able' for humans. What an object affords depends not only on the characteristics of the object, but also on the perspective of the animal. For example, a chair for a bird is not 'sit-on-able', rather it is 'stand-on-able'. Affordances thus link action to perception.

Gibson's concept of affordances stimulated work on the role of action in perception, and also highlighted the importance of ecologically valid information (in contrast to the simplified visual input used in many laboratories) (Gordon, 1989). However, the concept was also criticized for not explaining how experience changes animals, and for ignoring experimental work on visual processing (Gordon, 1989).

Perception as simulation

Möller (1996, 1999) suggested that the perception of shape (of an object) and space (surrounding an agent) is based on the simulation of actions and their sensory consequences. In this work, the one-way sensory processing is criticized to be unable to select behavior-relevant image structures, and further, to require an internal observer that needs to act upon a sensory representation to choose the appropriate behavior. As an alternative, perception is understood as anticipation. First, an agent learns the sensory consequences

---

[5]No experiment can show that *all* forms of perception depend on action. On the contrary, Goodale and Milner (1992) argued that visual processing has two different streams, only one of them relates to action. It is still possible though that these different streams strongly interact (Franz et al., 2003). How far the two streams actually differ is still debated.

of its motor commands. Then, it simulates covert motor commands to obtain the behavioral meaning of sensory information.

In a behavioral task, a series of actions is chosen due to an evaluation of the predicted sensory state. Based on this idea, Gross et al. (1999) let a mobile robot navigate collision-free through a maze. In a recognition task, just the outcome of a simulated action sequence is analyzed. For example, a mobile agent would recognize a situation as a dead-end by mentally simulating movements and by predicting that no movements are possible beyond the dead-end. Here, perception is not based on matching visual cues of the dead-end to a prototype stored in the brain. Thus, the approach has the potential to generalize over dead-ends of different appearance and to solve the problem of object constancy (that is, an object can be recognized independently of the perspective). Further, objects can be classified based on the outcome of the simulation.

Such an approach requires the brain to be able to simulate actions without causing movements, to simulate sensation without receiving sensory input, and to associate action with the resulting changes in sensation. Hesslow (2002) reviewed evidence for all three requirements[6]. He even suggested that internal simulation is a "mechanism for generating the inner world that we associate with consciousness" (p. 246).

The ideas of Grush (2004) go in the same direction. In addition, he claimed that the simulation of covert motor commands is not enough because the outcome of a motor command depends on the current proprioceptive state. Thus, a covert motor command should act on an 'emulator' of the body, which updates the simulated proprioceptive state. Such an emulator would, for example, explain the occurrence of a paralyzed phantom limb following pre-amputation paralysis: before the amputation, the emulator learned that any motor plan is mapped onto a constant proprioceptive state.

Consistent with all these simulation approaches are psychological experiments that show that action planning and perception (or sensory prediction) interfere with each other (Prinz, 1997; Wexler and Klam, 2001; Wohlschläger, 2001). Thus, action planning and perception seem to share a 'common representational domain' (Prinz, 1997). Such a common representation might lie in the mechanism of sensorimotor simulation.

A sensorimotor account of visual consciousness

According to O'Regan and Noë (2001), all awareness is based on mastering sensorimotor associations. They suggest that exercising these associations explains the perception of constancy and the difference between auditory

---

[6]The review is based on his concept of anticipation. There, a series of overt stimuli and overt responses is simulated.

and visual experience. As an example for the first, they argue that a line cannot be recognized solely by its sensory representation. The neural pattern in the visual cortex does not resemble a line anymore because on the retina, the photo receptors are distributed inhomogeneously, and furthermore, the mapping onto the visual cortex is non-linear. The line can be recognized, however, by exploiting its invariance; namely, a line shifted along its extension does not change its appearance. Thus, we perceive a line by knowing how the sensory input changes when we move along the line.

Visual and auditory sensory input vary in different and specific ways when the body moves. Therefore, knowing how the image of an object changes when we rotate it before our eyes might explain visual experience (O'Regan and Noë, 2001); "... the visual quality of shape is precisely the set of all potential distortions that the shape undergoes when it is moved relative to us, or when we move relative to it" (p. 942). Support for this claim comes from visuotactile devices made for the blind to 'see' (Bach-Y-Rita, 1972). Here, an image from a camera mounted near the eyes of a blind is transformed into a tactile pattern on an electrical stimulus matrix, which is mounted on the back or abdomen. After some training, the blind can recognize objects or step back from obstacles approaching the eyes (even if the stimulus occurs actually on his back). O'Regan and Noë (2001) therefore argue against special neurons or neural properties that cause visual awareness.

Overall, it is an appealing concept. So far, however, it does not provide a formalism explaining how the process works. Recently, Philipona et al. (2003, 2004) provided a formalism, but it only addresses the perception of the dimensionality of space, and qualities like object recognition are not addressed. Chapter 7 will come back to the idea about perceiving constancy.

1.5 Learning of sensorimotor models

The above sensorimotor approaches presume that an agent (robot) is equipped with an internal model of the relation between motor commands or movements and the resulting sensory states. In a behavior-based approach, the agent must learn this relation from experience. Such adaptive behavior can be achieved with neural networks, which are able to learn from examples and generalize between them. This section first gives a short overview of artificial neural networks, and then describes internal models. Finally, the last parts give an overview of existing learning paradigms for sensorimotor models: paradigms based on feed-forward networks, paradigms based on recurrent neural networks, and two extensions of the self-organizing-map algorithm (Kohonen, 1995).

1.5.1   Neural networks

Artificial neural networks are simplified models of neurons and their connections in the brain. This section just provides a classification of different structures and functions. The basic mathematics and applications can be found, for example, in Hertz et al. (1991) and Haykin (1998).

The structure of neural networks can be divided into two classes: feedforward networks and recurrent neural networks (figure 1.1). The first have connections in one direction from input to output. Here, the prominent type is the multi-layer perceptron (MLP). It has an input layer, one hidden layer or many hidden layers, and an output layer. MLPs approximate functions. Therefore, they map from one input pattern to just one output pattern (one-to-one or many-to-one mappings), but they fail on one-to-many mappings.

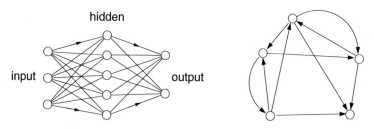

Figure 1.1: Two basic neural-network structures: feed-forward (left) and recurrent (right).

In contrast, recurrent neural networks have feed-back connections. Therefore, they do not approximate functions, instead their state (the values of all neurons) changes in time[7]. The convergence of the state depends on the connections. Partially recurrent networks that feed the network output back into the input oscillate. They have been used for time-series prediction. A prominent example is the Elman network (Elman, 1990). This network has an MLP structure with an additional context layer, which receives delayed input from the hidden layer and therefore acts like a memory (see also figure 1.5). Fully interconnected networks with symmetric weights converge to a stable state. These networks have been used for pattern completion (Hopfield, 1982). Patterns can be stored as stable states.

Neural networks learn either in a supervised way with a teacher, or unsupervised. In supervised learning, a teacher provides a target value (at the output) for every input value. Examples are error backpropagation for feed-

---

[7]In these networks, the time can be continuous or discrete. However, this thesis only considers discrete-time models.

forward networks and backpropagation-through-time for recurrent networks (Hertz et al., 1991). In contrast, unsupervised learning methods do not need target values. They either store training patterns (Hopfield network), or try to find structure in the training set. Structure can be found by assuming that the training patterns lie on a lower-dimensional manifold embedded in the pattern space. For example, an auto-associative network—an MLP whose input and output are identical—constrains the output to a manifold whose local dimensionality equals the number of neurons in the smallest hidden layer (Hertz et al., 1991; Kambhatla and Leen, 1997). Further, the self-organizing-map algorithm (Kohonen, 1995) fits a grid to the embedded manifold (see section 1.5.5). Finally, networks that do a 'principal component analysis' (Diamantaras and Kung, 1996) exploit that the variance of the patterns is restricted to a few principal directions (see section 2.1).

1.5.2 Internal models

A special application for neural networks are internal models, which relate motor commands to the sensory change that they cause. Two types can be distinguished (figure 1.2). First, a *forward model* predicts the effect of an action; that is, it maps the current sensory state S_t (at the time t) and motor command M_t onto the sensory state at the next time step, S_{t+1}. Second, an *inverse model* computes the motor command M_t required to change the sensory state toward a desired value S_{t+1}.

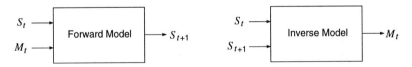

Figure 1.2: Internal models relate successive sensory states S_t and S_{t+1} with corresponding motor commands M_t.

In human physiology, internal models were suggested to be an integral part of motor control (Kawato et al., 1987; Wolpert et al., 1995). For goal-directed movements, inverse models are necessary to directly compute motor commands. On the other hand, forward models can predict an outcome of an action before the sensory feedback (via the environment) is available. Moreover, they might be used to cancel the sensory effects of movements (Blakemore et al., 2000) and to predict the consequences of actions without overtly executing them (Wolpert et al., 1995). Chapter 7 will use a forward model for prediction.

1.5.3   Feed-forward networks as internal models

This section describes internal models that are built with multi-layer perceptrons. Forward models can be learned by observing the effect $\hat{S}_{t+1}$ of actions M_t on the environment. This effect $\hat{S}_{t+1}$ is the target value in the training (Jordan and Rumelhart, 1992).

For inverse models, actions and effects exchange their role as input and output. One approach to learn an inverse model is 'direct inverse modeling' (Jordan and Rumelhart, 1992). Here, the environment produces input patterns instead of target values (figure 1.3). The action M_t will result in the sensory state $\hat{S}_{t+1}$. Thus, the inverse model can be trained to map $\hat{S}_{t+1}$ onto M_t. Training data can be produced by randomly sampling the action space (Kuperstein, 1988).

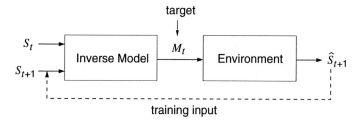

Figure 1.3: Direct inverse modeling.

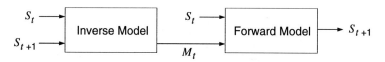

Figure 1.4: Distal supervised learning.

However, this approach will fail if the environment maps different motor commands onto the same sensory state. The inverse model cannot learn the corresponding one-to-many mapping because the MLP would average across the many possible motor commands, and such an average might not be a desirable solution (Movellan and McClelland, 1993). Therefore, Jordan and Rumelhart (1992) suggested to link the inverse model with a forward model (figure 1.4). First, the forward model is trained separately, as described above. Then, the combined network learns an identity mapping (note, in figure 1.4, S_{t+1} acts both as an input and as a target). In the learning process, the weights of the inverse model are adjusted using error backpropagation, while the error propagates through the forward model without changing its weights.

1.5.4 Recurrent neural networks as internal models

This section presents two sets of examples showing how recurrent neural networks can be applied. The first set exploits the recurrent connection to predict a series of sensory states, and the second set uses the relaxation to stable points for an associative task.

Tani (1996) used a partially recurrent neural network with a context layer (figure 1.5) as a forward model for a mobile robot. The robot's environment was separated into paths and intersections by obstacles. Here, the sensory state was a set of distances to obstacles, and the motor command, which was binary, represented the path of choice at an intersection. Using backpropagation-through-time, the recurrent network was trained on series of sensory states and corresponding motor commands. After training, given a sequence of motor commands, the network could predict the resulting sensory state.

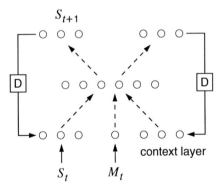

Figure 1.5: Recurrent neural network with context layer. At each time step the network maps the current sensory state S_t and motor command M_t onto the succeeding sensory state S_{t+1}. Dashed arrows indicate complete connections between two layers. The boxes labeled D delay the feedback by one time step.

The trained network was also applied to a planning task. Here, the sequence of motor commands is not known, but the final desired sensory state is known. Tani (1996) solved this problem by defining a cost function based on the difference between the desired state and the predicted state that results from a motor sequence. The motor commands were obtained by minimizing this cost function using gradient descent.

In a simulation of a mobile robot, Jirenhed et al. (2001) also used a recurrent neural network for prediction. Here, the environment contained corridors and corners, but no intersections. The robot had two wheels, whose velocities were the motor commands. Instead of having these motor commands as a network input, they were predicted. The goal of this study was to show that the robot can simulate its movement through the environment. Jirenhed et al. (2001) interpreted this simulation as an emerging 'inner world'.

Cruse and Steinkühler (1993) showed that the relaxation in a recurrent neural network can be used to solve the inverse kinematics of a redundant robot arm (which can adopt many postures for a given end-effector position). A simulated robot arm was composed of three line segments in the plane. The geometric relations of the arm-joint positions were put into a redundant set of linear equations, $s = As$, with the unknown state s. This set of equations can be represented by a recurrent neural network, interpreting the matrix A as a set of weights (figure 1.6). Such a network can complete a partially given state. Any component of the state vector s can be set equal to the corresponding component of an input vector x, which is fixed in its values. The output is computed by iterating the state s,

$$s_i(t+1) = \sum_j A_{ij} \left([1 - g_j]s_j(t) + g_j x_j \right) \ , \tag{1.1}$$

with $g_j = 1$ for input components and $g_j = 0$ for output components. The state relaxes to a stable point, which yields the output values.

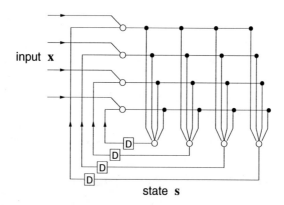

Figure 1.6: Recurrent neural network that iterates a state vector s, given an input x. Neurons are drawn as circles, and synapses (weights) as black dots. The boxes labeled D delay the feedback by one time step.

This approach was further extended to non-linear equations (using the non-linear functions as activation functions) and to an arm in three-dimensions with six degrees of freedom (Steinkühler and Cruse, 1998). The application is not limited to a robot arm; a recurrent network can be also built for landmark navigation if the coordinates of the landmarks and of the goal are given (Cruse, 2003b). Cruse (2001) argued that recurrent networks are much more plausible to describe brain function because they allow the animal to obtain an internal state and memory, and thus let the animal escape from being a purely reactive system. In addition, Cruse (2003a) related the recall in recurrent networks, as described above, to the emergence of an internal world.

1.5.5 Self-organizing maps

To learn sensorimotor relations, Ritter et al. (1990) used the self-organizing map (SOM) algorithm (Kohonen, 1995). This algorithm fits a q-dimensional grid to a distribution of training patterns in $\mathbb{R}^d$, $q \leq d$ (Kohonen, 1982). SOMs were motivated by sensory maps in the brain, for example, the somatosensory map or the tonotopic map (Kohonen, 1989). A SOM consists of a q-dimensional array[8] of nodes; each node i has a location $\mathbf{r}_i$ and a weight vector $\mathbf{w}_i$ (figure 1.7). The weight vectors are in the space of the training patterns.

The algorithm consists of three steps, which are alternated until convergence is reached. First, a training pattern $\mathbf{x}$ is drawn randomly. Second, the node c is determined whose weight vector $\mathbf{w}_c$ is closest to $\mathbf{x}$,

$$c = \arg\min_i \|\mathbf{x} - \mathbf{w}_i\| \ . \tag{1.2}$$

Third, all weights are updated, depending on each nodes distance $\|\mathbf{r}_i - \mathbf{r}_c\|$ to the best matching node c,

$$\mathbf{w}_i(t+1) = \mathbf{w}_i(t) + h_{ic}\left[\mathbf{x}(t) - \mathbf{w}_i(t)\right] \quad \forall i \ . \tag{1.3}$$

The neighborhood function h_{ic} is

$$h_{ic} = \alpha(t) \exp\left(-\frac{\|\mathbf{r}_i - \mathbf{r}_c\|^2}{2\sigma^2(t)}\right) \ . \tag{1.4}$$

The learning rate $\alpha(t)$ and the radius of the neighborhood $\sigma(t)$ both decrease monotonically in time t. The neighborhood function ensures that the grid of

---

[8]Here, for simplicity, the discussion is limited to square grids, which are the most common, but the algorithm is not restricted to them; for example, hexagonal grids were also used (Kohonen, 1995).

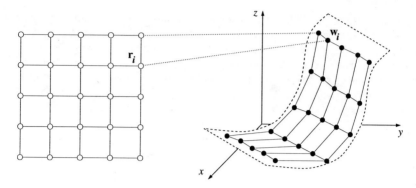

Figure 1.7: Node locations (left: circles) and weight vectors (right: black dots). Each node i with location $\mathbf{r}_i$ has an associated weight vector $\mathbf{w}_i$ in the space of training patterns (dotted lines mark sample associations). The dashed lines and curves indicate the manifold of training patterns.

weights has the same topology as the array of nodes. If the training patterns lie on a q-dimensional manifold, the algorithm makes the grid of weights to follow this manifold (figure 1.7, right). Many examples can be found in Kohonen (1995).

The SOM algorithm can be easily extended by adding more parameters to each node and by updating them in parallel to the weight vectors. With such an extension, Ritter and Schulten (1986) used the SOM to learn sensorimotor relations. Here, a training pattern consists of a pair $(\mathbf{x},\mathbf{y})$ of sensor values $\mathbf{x}$ and corresponding motor values $\mathbf{y}$. Such a sensorimotor pattern is an element in the space formed by the Cartesian product of the sensor and the motor space. The SOM extension has two weight vectors for each node i, one for the sensory input, $\mathbf{w}_i^{\text{in}}$, and one for the motor output, $\mathbf{w}_i^{\text{out}}$. The computation (1.2) of the best matching node is restricted to the sensory domain; but both $\mathbf{w}_i^{\text{in}}$ and $\mathbf{w}_i^{\text{out}}$ are updated according to (1.3) ($\mathbf{w}_i^{\text{out}}$ is updated based on $\mathbf{y}$, and the neighborhood function may have different parameters).

This algorithm fits the grid of weight vectors $(\mathbf{w}_i^{\text{in}}, \mathbf{w}_i^{\text{out}})$ to the sensorimotor pattern distribution. The resulting link between a sensory input $\mathbf{w}_i^{\text{in}}$ and a motor output $\mathbf{w}_i^{\text{out}}$ provides a discrete mapping, usable for an inverse model. To obtain a continuous mapping, Ritter et al. (1989) further added a locally linear map to each node. The result was successfully applied to control a robot arm with three degrees of freedom.

The restriction of the node competition (1.2) to the distance in sensory space reduces the search space for the weights, but it makes the approach fail

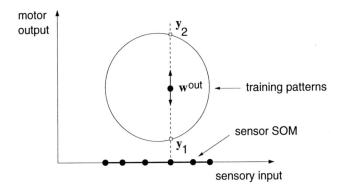

Figure 1.8: Failure of the sensorimotor extension of SOM on one-to-many mappings. The motor component $\mathbf{w}^{\text{out}}$ is averaged over competing patterns $\mathbf{y}_1$ and $\mathbf{y}_2$.

on one-to-many mappings (figure 1.8). The learning for $\mathbf{w}_i^{\text{in}}$ is independent of $\mathbf{w}_i^{\text{out}}$. As a result, a classical SOM algorithm is applied solely to the sensory domain, while $\mathbf{w}_i^{\text{out}}$ is updated simultaneously. In the case of two possible target values for one sensory input, $\mathbf{w}_i^{\text{out}}$ is attracted to two different positions $\mathbf{y}_1$ and $\mathbf{y}_2$ (because the node competition is independent of the distance to $\mathbf{y}_1$ or $\mathbf{y}_2$). Thus, as a result from the update rule (1.3), $\mathbf{w}_i^{\text{out}}$ will be averaged among $\mathbf{y}_1$ and $\mathbf{y}_2$. For example, given that both $\mathbf{y}_1$ and $\mathbf{y}_2$ are drawn with the same probability ($p = 0.5$), on average, $\mathbf{w}_i^{\text{out}}$ is updated according to

$$
\begin{aligned}
\mathbf{w}_i^{\text{out}}(t+1) &= \mathbf{w}_i^{\text{out}}(t) + \frac{1}{2}h_{ic}\left[\mathbf{y}_1 - \mathbf{w}_i^{\text{out}}(t)\right] + \frac{1}{2}h_{ic}\left[\mathbf{y}_2 - \mathbf{w}_i^{\text{out}}(t)\right] \\
&= \mathbf{w}_i^{\text{out}}(t) + h_{ic}\left[\frac{1}{2}(\mathbf{y}_1 + \mathbf{y}_2) - \mathbf{w}_i^{\text{out}}(t)\right] .
\end{aligned}
\tag{1.5}
$$

Therefore, the resulting relation between sensory input and motor output is invalid.

Further limitations arise from the SOM grid structure. First, since sensorimotor manifolds are usually non-linear, many grid points are needed. With increasing dimensionality q of the manifold, the number of necessary points increases exponentially (the number of points per dimension to the power of q). Soon ($q > 3$), this gets computationally unfeasible. As a solution to this problem, Martinetz and Schulten (1990) suggested an extension to hierarchical SOM. A second limitation arises in real world applications: some sensor values could be pure noise (or irrelevant to the sensorimotor map). Such noise dimensions need to be filled with grid points (figure 1.9), resulting in the same problems as mentioned above.

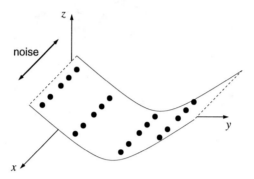

Figure 1.9: Noise (in x direction) extends a one-dimensional relation between y and z (solid curve) to a two-dimensional manifold. The grid points (black dots) need to fill the whole manifold.

1.5.6   Parametrized self-organizing maps

Ritter (1993) presented an extension to the above SOM approach for learning sensorimotor maps, the 'parametrized self-organizing map' (PSOM). The PSOM can cope with kinematic models of redundant robot arms (Walter et al., 2000). I first describe the training phase and then the recall phase.

The PSOM assumes that the training patterns lie on a sensorimotor manifold. In training, a continuous mapping is constructed that maps a parameter space (resembling the array in the SOM) onto the sensorimotor manifold. As for the SOM, the parameter space is based on an array of nodes $\mathbf{r}_i$, and each node i has a weight vector $\mathbf{w}_i \in \mathbb{R}^d$ (here, element in the sensorimotor space). A continuous mapping from $\mathbf{r}$ to $\mathbf{w}$ is achieved by a sum of basis functions $H_i(\mathbf{r})$ (one for each node i),

$$\mathbf{w}(\mathbf{r}) = \sum_i H_i(\mathbf{r})\mathbf{w}_i \ . \tag{1.6}$$

These basis functions are predefined and fulfill $H_i(\mathbf{r}_j) = \delta_{ij} \ \forall i, j$ (Ritter, 1993). Thus, the mapping interpolates between the given grid points $\mathbf{w}_i$. Different from the SOM extension in section 1.5.5, only a few grid points are needed to describe a non-linear sensorimotor manifold. The grids usually have a side length of three points (Walter et al., 2000). In applications, mostly the motor components (for example, the joint angles of a robot arm) are chosen to form the parameter space, which further needs to be equidistantly sampled (Walter et al., 2000). The corresponding sensor values can be gained by executing the motor commands (or by taking the posture given by the joint angles).

The recall works like a pattern completion. The completion of a vector $\mathbf{x}$ is gained by finding the parameter $\mathbf{r}$ that minimizes the distance between $\mathbf{x}$ and the sensorimotor manifold $\mathbf{w}(\mathbf{r})$. Since $\mathbf{x}$ is only partially given, only the distance to the input components is evaluated,

$$\mathbf{r}_{\min} = \arg\min_{\mathbf{r}} \sum_{j=1}^{d} g_j (x_j - w_j(\mathbf{r}))^2 \ . \tag{1.7}$$

Here, $g_j > 0$ for input components, and $g_j = 0$ for output components. The minimization needs to be solved numerically (Ritter, 1993; Walter et al., 2000).

This recall method has the advantage that it works in any direction. Thus, for example, a forward model can be changed into an inverse model by adjusting the g_j values. Further, the method can be applied to redundant robot arms. Out of many possible postures, the one with the smallest distance to the manifold $\mathbf{w}(\mathbf{r})$ is chosen, and not an average as in section 1.5.5.

The PSOM algorithm can achieve a remarkable accuracy (for example, a mean deviation of 1% of the working space for a three degrees-of-freedom robot finger (Walter et al., 2000)), but also here limitations exist. First, we need to know the topology of the sensorimotor patterns. Second, the mapping $\mathbf{w}(\mathbf{r})$ requires a smooth sensorimotor manifold. Third, as in the previous approach, it is not clear how the algorithm can cope with noise dimensions.

Chapter 2

Modeling of data distributions

The data we try to model are patterns whose coordinates include all sensory variables and all motor variables[1]. The set of these patterns forms a distribution in a sensorimotor space. In this thesis, the focus is on finding a simplified representation of such a distribution. That is, learning is based on finding a statistical description of the data, instead of constructing a neural network. Like a network, however, the proposed algorithms will have a training phase, in which the distribution is approximated, and a recall phase, in which a partially given input pattern is completed, as in a recurrent neural network (section 1.5.4). These training and recall phases can be also found in the self-organizing map (section 1.5.5) and the parameterized self-organizing map (section 1.5.6). Different from these algorithms, however, the present approach is based on principal component analysis (PCA). Since PCA can only give a linear approximation of a data distribution, two extensions are used. The first extends the single PCA to a mixture of many analyzers. Here, each analyzer approximates linearly a locally confined region of the pattern space. This restriction of PCA is called 'local PCA'. PCA itself cannot separate the space into these regions. The separation is accomplished by linking local PCA to vector quantization. The second extension (kernel PCA) uses only one analyzer, but approximates linearly the data in a higher-dimensional space into which they were mapped. This chapter describes the background of these two extensions.

2.1 Principal component analysis (PCA)

Principal component analysis is a widely used tool for dimension reduction (Diamantaras and Kung, 1996). Let $\mathbf{x}_i \in \mathbb{R}^d$, where $i = 1, \ldots, n$, be the training patterns. The principal components are a set of $q < d$ orthonormal

---

[1]In this thesis, the 'motor variables' may also be proprioception, like, for example, the posture of a robot arm.

vectors and span a subspace in the major directions into which the patterns extend (figure 2.1).

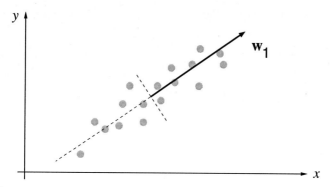

Figure 2.1: The principal component $\mathbf{w}_1$ points into the direction of maximum variance. The gray dots are the training patterns. The intersection of the dashed lines is the center of the pattern distribution.

In this section, we assume that the patterns are centered around the origin (without loss of generality). Let $\mathbf{y}$ be the projection onto a subspace,

$$\mathbf{y} = \mathbf{W}^T \mathbf{x} \ . \tag{2.1}$$

$\mathbf{W}$ is a $d \times q$ matrix that contains the principal components as columns. The vector $\mathbf{y}$ is a dimension-reduced representation of $\mathbf{x}$. Let $\hat{\mathbf{x}}$ be the reconstruction of $\mathbf{x}$ given only the vector $\mathbf{y}$,

$$\hat{\mathbf{x}} = \mathbf{W}\mathbf{y} \ . \tag{2.2}$$

The goal of PCA is to set the subspace such that the mean reconstruction error E_{rec} is minimized,

$$E_{\text{rec}} = \frac{1}{n} \sum_{i=1}^{n} \|\mathbf{x}_i - \hat{\mathbf{x}}_i\|^2 \ . \tag{2.3}$$

This goal is equivalent to finding the q major directions of maximal variance within the set of patterns $\{\mathbf{x}_i\}$ (Diamantaras and Kung, 1996). Moreover, it is equivalent to the principal components being the first q eigenvectors $\mathbf{w}_l$ of the covariance matrix $\mathbf{C}$ of the pattern set (Diamantaras and Kung, 1996),

$$\mathbf{C} = \frac{1}{n} \sum_{i=1}^{n} \mathbf{x}_i \mathbf{x}_i^T \ . \tag{2.4}$$

The corresponding eigenvalue equation is

$$\mathbf{C}\mathbf{w}_l = \lambda_l \mathbf{w}_l \ . \tag{2.5}$$

The eigenvalue λ_l is the variance of the distribution $\{\mathbf{x}_i\}$ in the direction of $\mathbf{w}_l$. The following sections describe how neural networks can extract principal components and how PCA can be linked to the probability density of a pattern distribution.

2.1.1 Neural networks for PCA

Principal components can be extracted using single-layer feed-forward neural networks (Oja, 1989; Sanger, 1989; Rubner and Tavan, 1989; Diamantaras and Kung, 1996). These networks learn unsupervised by using variants of the Hebbian rule. They provide an iterative solution to (2.5) and do not need the computation of $\mathbf{C}$, which could be computationally expensive (it is $O(d^2 n)$). Networks extracting principal components further provide a biological basis for PCA. One example of such a PCA algorithm is Oja's rule.

Oja's algorithm (Oja, 1982) uses a single neuron with an input vector $\mathbf{x}$, a weight vector $\mathbf{w}$, and an output y. The output can be written as $y = \mathbf{w}^T\mathbf{x}$ (this corresponds to (2.1)). According to Oja's rule, after a training pattern $\mathbf{x}$ is presented, the weights change by a Hebbian term minus a forgetting function:

$$\mathbf{w}(t+1) = \mathbf{w}(t) + \varepsilon y \mathbf{x} - \alpha y^2 \mathbf{w}(t) \tag{2.6}$$

ε is the Hebbian learning rate, and α is a constant. The forgetting term is necessary to bound the magnitude of $\mathbf{w}$. For the average update over all training patterns $\mathbf{x}_i$, the fixed points of (2.6) can be computed. In turns out that they are the eigenvectors of the covariance matrix $\mathbf{C}$, and the eigenvector with the largest eigenvalue is the only stable point (Oja, 1982). Thus, Oja's rule extracts the principal component.

2.1.2 Probabilistic PCA

Probabilistic PCA links PCA to the probability density of patterns $\mathbf{x}_i$ (Tipping and Bishop, 1997). The given set $\{\mathbf{x}_i\}$ is assumed to originate from a probability density $p(\mathbf{x})$. Further, $\mathbf{x}$ is assumed to be a linear combination of a vector $\mathbf{y} \in \mathbb{R}^q$ with density $p(\mathbf{y})$ and a noise vector $\mathbf{e} \in \mathbb{R}^d$ with density $p(\mathbf{e})$,

$$\mathbf{x} = \mathbf{U}\mathbf{y} + \mathbf{e} \ . \tag{2.7}$$

The goal is to find $\mathbf{U}$, which is a $d \times q$ matrix. Both densities $p(\mathbf{y})$ and $p(\mathbf{e})$ are assumed to be uniformly Gaussian with variance one respective σ^2. Thus, the density $p(\mathbf{x})$ is defined uniquely up to the parameters $\mathbf{U}$ and σ,

$$p(\mathbf{x}) = (2\pi)^{-d/2}(\det \mathbf{B})^{-1/2} \exp\left(-\frac{1}{2}\mathbf{x}^T \mathbf{B}^{-1}\mathbf{x}\right) \tag{2.8}$$

with $\mathbf{B} = \sigma^2\mathbf{I} + \mathbf{U}\mathbf{U}^T$ (Tipping and Bishop, 1997). Probabilistic PCA determines $\mathbf{U}$ and σ such that the patterns $\mathbf{x}_i$ if drawn from $p(\mathbf{x})$ are most likely (Tipping and Bishop, 1997). That is, the likelihood, which is

$$L = \prod_{i=1}^{n} p(\mathbf{x}_i) \ , \tag{2.9}$$

is maximized (see appendix A.2 for an example of the maximum likelihood principle). The result of this optimization gives the matrix $\mathbf{U}$ (Tipping and Bishop, 1997),

$$\mathbf{U} = \mathbf{W}(\mathbf{\Lambda} - \sigma^2\mathbf{I})^{1/2}\mathbf{R} \ . \tag{2.10}$$

The columns of the matrix $\mathbf{W}$ are the eigenvectors of the covariance matrix of $\{\mathbf{x}_i\}$; the diagonal matrix $\mathbf{\Lambda}$ contains the corresponding eigenvalues, and $\mathbf{R}$ is an arbitrary rotational matrix (note, $\mathbf{y}$ has a uniform Gaussian distribution). The noise variance σ^2 turns out to be the residual variance per dimension,

$$\sigma^2 = \frac{1}{d-q}\sum_{l=q+1}^{d} \lambda_l \ . \tag{2.11}$$

To evaluate (2.11), only the q principal eigenvalues and the total variance (sum of variances over all dimensions, which equals the trace of the covariance matrix) need to be known. It is not necessary to compute the $d - q$ minor principal components. Thus, the introduction of the noise allows the density $p(\mathbf{x})$ to be defined over the whole $\mathbb{R}^d$, while using a reduced parameter set (obtained by PCA). Equation (2.11) shows how fast $p(\mathbf{x})$ decreases orthogonal to the subspace spanned by the principal components.

2.2   Vector quantization

Vector quantization describes a pattern set using a reduced number of so-called 'code-book' vectors. We assume again that n training patterns $\mathbf{x}_i \in \mathbb{R}^d$ are given. Let $m < n$ be the number of code-book vectors $\mathbf{c}_j \in \mathbb{R}^d$. In the final state, each training pattern is assigned to one code-book vector. The optimal position of code-book vectors is usually gained by finding the minimum of the sum E of squared distances[2] between each code-book vector and its assigned patterns,

$$E = \sum_{ij} P(j|\mathbf{x}_i) \|\mathbf{x}_i - \mathbf{c}_j\|^2 \ . \tag{2.12}$$

$P(j|\mathbf{x}_i)$ is the probability that $\mathbf{x}_i$ belongs to $\mathbf{c}_j$. For the final state, $P(j|\mathbf{x}_i) = 1$ if $\mathbf{x}_i$ is assigned to $\mathbf{c}_j$, and $P(j|\mathbf{x}_i) = 0$ otherwise. A pattern is assigned to the code-book vector that has the smallest Euclidean distance to that pattern. Thus, the code-book vectors induce a Voronoi tessellation of space (figure 2.2). In each of the separated regions, the position of the code-book vector is the center-of-mass of the local pattern distribution (otherwise (2.12) cannot be minimal).

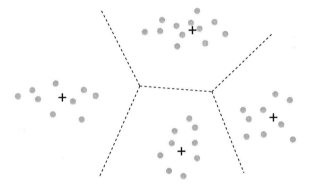

Figure 2.2: Code-book vectors (crosses) and the resulting Voronoi tessellation (dashed lines are boundaries, equidistant from two respective codebook vectors). Training patterns are drawn as gray dots.

The difficulty in finding the optimal $\{\mathbf{c}_j\}$ is that E has many local minima. No general solution exists. Instead, various iterative algorithms exist that find approximate solutions. The algorithms can be divided into those that use hard-clustering and those that use soft-clustering. In hard-clustering, $P(j|\mathbf{x}_i)$ is binary (throughout the iteration), and each $\mathbf{x}_i$ can be only assigned to one code-book vector. In soft-clustering, $P(j|\mathbf{x}_i)$ can take any value in the interval [0;1].

---

[2]Here, the discussion is limited to the Euclidean distance, other measures like the Holder norm, or the Minkowski norm were also used (Linde et al., 1980).

The algorithms can be further divided into on-line and batch versions. On-line versions update code-book vectors in each iteration step based on just one (randomly drawn) training pattern $\mathbf{x}_i$ (as for the self-organizing map, section 1.5.5). The update rule is usually written as

$$\mathbf{c}_j(t+1) = \mathbf{c}_j(t) + \varepsilon(t)P(j|\mathbf{x}_i)\left[\mathbf{x}_i - \mathbf{c}_j(t)\right] \ . \tag{2.13}$$

The change of $\mathbf{c}_j$ is in the direction of the negative gradient of (2.12). $\varepsilon(t)$ is a learning rate, which can depend on time. In contrast, batch versions use all training patterns for each step. Here, the algorithm alternates between computing all $P(j|\mathbf{x}_i)$ based on a given distribution $\{\mathbf{c}_j\}$, and optimizing all $\mathbf{c}_j$ given $P(j|\mathbf{x}_i)$. This algorithm is a variant of the expectation maximization algorithm (Dempster et al., 1977). The 'maximization' step is a minimization of the error E (which maximizes the likelihood, see section 2.3.1).

The following sections describe the hard-clustering algorithm 'k-means' and provide more details about soft-clustering algorithms. Two examples are described: 'deterministic annealing' and 'Neural Gas'.

2.2.1   K-means

The most used hard-clustering algorithm is k-means (Lloyd, 1982; Moody and Darken, 1989). Here, in each iteration step, first, based on the Voronoi tessellation, for all j, $P(j|\mathbf{x}_i)$ is calculated for one $\mathbf{x}_i$ (on-line version) or all patterns (batch version). Then, in the on-line version, the code-book assigned to $\mathbf{x}_i$ is moved closer to $\mathbf{x}_i$ (using (2.13) with $\varepsilon(t) = \varepsilon$). In the batch version, each $\mathbf{c}_j$ is moved to the center of its assigned patterns (which minimizes (2.12) given the assignment $P(j|\mathbf{x}_i)$). These steps are repeated until convergence is reached. The disadvantage of k-means is that it is prone to end at a local minimum, and therefore, its success depends on the initial choice of $\{\mathbf{c}_j\}$.

2.2.2   Soft-clustering

In soft-clustering, many code-book vectors compete for one pattern $\mathbf{x}_i$. A common assignment $P(j|\mathbf{x}_i)$ is the normalized Gaussian function (see, for example, Yair et al. (1992)),

$$P(j|\mathbf{x}_i) = \frac{\exp\left(-\beta\|\mathbf{x}_i - \mathbf{c}_j\|^2\right)}{\sum_j \exp\left(-\beta\|\mathbf{x}_i - \mathbf{c}_j\|^2\right)} \ . \tag{2.14}$$

The parameter β controls the influence range of a pattern $\mathbf{x}_i$ or code-book vector. For the limit $\beta \to \infty$, the algorithm is the same as hard-clustering. $P(j|\mathbf{x}_i)$ is normalized such that $\sum_j P(j|\mathbf{x}_i) = 1$ (this allows a probabilistic interpretation). Equation (2.14) can be derived using the maximum entropy principle. From all possible sets $\{P(j|\mathbf{x}_i)\}$ that result in a given total cost E according to (2.12), the Gibbs distribution (2.14) maximizes the entropy (Rose et al., 1990). Thus, the assignment (2.14) does not rely on any assumptions about the distribution of patterns. In this physical perspective, β has the role of an inverse temperature. The soft-clustering approach can be extended to an annealing process, which helps to avoid local minima (Rose et al., 1990).

2.2.3 Deterministic annealing

Deterministic annealing extends soft-clustering to an annealing process (Rose et al., 1990; Rose, 1998). For each temperature value, the algorithm iterates between the calculation of all $P(j|\mathbf{x}_i)$ and the update of the code-book vectors (in batch mode), until convergence is reached. The annealing starts with a high temperature (low β). Here, all code-book vectors converge to the center of the pattern distribution (independent of their initial positions). Below a critical temperature the vectors start to split. Further decreasing the temperature (increasing β) leads to more splittings until all code-book vectors are separate. The annealing can therefore avoid (if it is sufficiently slow) the convergence to local minima of (2.12). Deterministic annealing is originally formulated as batch method, but also an on-line version exists (Qiu et al., 1994).

2.2.4 Neural Gas

Martinetz et al. (1993) presented an algorithm called 'Neural Gas' that outperforms deterministic annealing (Rose et al., 1990). Neural Gas is also a variant of soft-clustering, and it also uses annealing. In contrast, Neural Gas has a different (heuristic) assignment, and it can be only carried out as an on-line version.

The algorithm starts by randomly choosing m data points as starting points for the m code-book vectors. The annealing consists of a predefined number of $t_{\max}$ steps. During each annealing step t, a pattern $\mathbf{x}_i$ is randomly drawn from the training set. Then, the code-book vectors are sorted in the order of their Euclidean distance to $\mathbf{x}_i$. Let $k(\mathbf{x}_i, \mathbf{c}_j(t))$ be the resulting rank of each code-book vector, with $k = 0$ for the closest vector, and $k = m - 1$ for the most distant vector. The soft-assignment is then given by the function $h_\varrho^{ij} = \exp(-k(\mathbf{x}_i, \mathbf{c}_j(t))/\varrho)$. The parameter ϱ is a measure of the neighborhood range. Given this assignment, all code-book vectors $\mathbf{c}_j$ are updated according to

$$\mathbf{c}_j(t+1) = \mathbf{c}_j(t) + \varepsilon(t) h_{\varrho(t)}^{ij} \left[\mathbf{x}_i - \mathbf{c}_j(t) \right] \quad . \tag{2.15}$$

During the annealing process both parameters ε and ϱ decrease exponentially, $\varrho(t) = \varrho(0)[\varrho(t_{\max})/\varrho(0)]^{(t/t_{\max})}$, and $\varepsilon(t) = \varepsilon(0)[\varepsilon(t_{\max})/\varepsilon(0)]^{(t/t_{\max})}$. At the end of the annealing, the algorithm changes to on-line k-means, and thus, also (locally) minimizes (2.12). The exponential decay of ε enforces convergence. Neural Gas is stable and does not depend on the initial configuration of $\{\mathbf{c}_i\}$ (Martinetz et al., 1993).

2.3   Mixture of local PCA

A mixture of local PCA combines vector quantization with PCA. Code-book vectors are replaced by local PCA units. Each unit has a center, and the PCA needs to be computed relative to this center. The principal components point into the directions of major variance of the local distribution of assigned patterns. Different from vector quantization, here no general cost function exists. Some algorithms (Hinton et al., 1997; Kambhatla and Leen, 1997) try to minimize a global reconstruction error, which is the sum over the reconstruction error (2.3) for each unit. Other algorithms use a mixture of Gaussian functions to model the density of the training data, and therefore, choose the parameters such that the likelihood of the data is maximized (Bishop, 1995).

The first group of algorithms assigns a pattern to the unit that reconstructs the pattern with a minimal error (2.3). Thus also distant patterns are assigned to a unit as long as they lie in the direction of the principal components. However, for modeling non-linear manifolds this is of a disadvantage because the units are not locally confined and protrude out of the manifold (Tipping and Bishop, 1999; Möller and Hoffmann, 2004). On the other hand, density models are locally confined and are discussed in the following.

2.3.1   Gaussian mixture models

Gaussian mixture models assume that the patterns $\mathbf{x}_i$ origin from a probability density $p(\mathbf{x})$ (Bishop, 1995). This density is a linear combination of Gaussian functions $p(\mathbf{x}|j)$,

$$p(\mathbf{x}|j) = \frac{1}{N_j} \exp\left(-\frac{1}{2}(\mathbf{x} - \mathbf{c}_j)^T \mathbf{A}_j (\mathbf{x} - \mathbf{c}_j) \right) \quad . \tag{2.16}$$

The normalization constant N_j is chosen such that the integral of $p(\mathbf{x}|j)$ over $\mathbb{R}^d$ equals one (a necessary condition for a probability density). The negative exponent is a weighted squared distance (called Mahalanobis distance) between $\mathbf{x}$ and the center $\mathbf{c}_j$; the corresponding weights are given by the symmetric matrix $\mathbf{A}_j$. The boundary that has a Mahalanobis distance to the center $\mathbf{c}_j$ equal to one is a hyper-ellipsoid.

The density $p(\mathbf{x})$ is a weighted sum of the local densities $p(\mathbf{x}|j)$,

$$p(\mathbf{x}) = \sum_{j=1}^{m} P(j)p(\mathbf{x}|j) \ . \tag{2.17}$$

To normalize $p(\mathbf{x})$, the weights $P(j)$ must sum to one, $\sum_{j=1}^{m} P(j) = 1$. Therefore, $P(j)$ can be interpreted as the probability that patterns originate from the unit j. It is called prior probability.

The goal of the mixture model is to find the unknown parameters $\mathbf{c}_j$, $\mathbf{A}_j$, and the priors $P(j)$ for each unit j such that the likelihood, $L = \prod_{i=1}^{n} p(\mathbf{x}_i)$, to obtain the distribution $\{\mathbf{x}_i\}$ given the density $p(\mathbf{x})$ is maximal (Bishop, 1995). To solve this optimization problem it is common to use a variant of the expectation maximization algorithm (Bishop, 1995). It consists of two steps with iterate until convergence is reached. In the expectation step, the soft-assignment $P(j|\mathbf{x}_i)$ for all j and i is computed based on a given estimate of the parameters $\mathbf{c}_j$, $\mathbf{A}_j$, and $P(j)$. $P(j|\mathbf{x}_i)$ is called posterior probability. It is computed using Bayes' theorem (see appendix A.1),

$$P(j|\mathbf{x}_i) = \frac{p(\mathbf{x}_i|j)P(j)}{p(\mathbf{x}_i)} \ . \tag{2.18}$$

In the special case of uniform Gaussians that all have the same width and weight $P(j)$, (2.18) is the same as the Gibbs distribution (2.14).

In the maximization step, the Gaussian's parameters $\mathbf{c}_j$, $\mathbf{A}_j$, and $P(j)$ that maximize the likelihood given all $P(j|\mathbf{x}_i)$ can be directly computed (Bishop, 1995). The result is that the center $\mathbf{c}_j$ is the weighted mean of the set $\{\mathbf{x}_i\}$,

$$\mathbf{c}_j = \frac{\sum_{i=1}^{n} P(j|\mathbf{x}_i)\mathbf{x}_i}{\sum_{i=1}^{n} P(j|\mathbf{x}_i)} \ , \tag{2.19}$$

and the matrix $\mathbf{A}_j$ is the inverse of the weighted covariance matrix $\mathbf{C}_j$,

$$\mathbf{C}_j = \frac{\sum_{i=1}^{n} P(j|\mathbf{x}_i)(\mathbf{x}_i - \mathbf{c}_j)(\mathbf{x}_i - \mathbf{c}_j)^T}{\sum_{i=1}^{n} P(j|\mathbf{x}_i)} \ . \tag{2.20}$$

The inverse can be computed by extracting all eigenvectors of $\mathbf{C}_j$. Thus, the axes of the mentioned hyper-ellipsoid are the principal components of the local data distribution. The size of this hyper-ellipsoid is given by the eigenvalues λ_j^l from the PCA (the semi-axis length of unit j in the direction l equals $\sqrt{\lambda_j^l}$). Finally, the result for the prior probabilities is

$$P(j) = \frac{1}{n} \sum_{i=1}^{n} P(j|\mathbf{x}_i) \ . \tag{2.21}$$

It can be shown that alternating these expectation and maximization steps increases the likelihood L in each iteration step (Bishop, 1995). However, local maxima are not avoided. Further, single isolated data points (outliers) can make the algorithm unstable (Archambeau et al., 2003). If just one pattern is assigned to a unit (that is, the other patterns have almost zero $P(j|\mathbf{x}_i)$) the variance of the local Gaussian collapses to zero. As an improvement to the local minima problem, annealing schemes (as discussed for the vector quantization, section 2.2) were suggested (Meinicke, 2000; Albrecht et al., 2000; Meinicke and Ritter, 2001). Here, a global variance linked to the width of each Gaussian is gradually reduced during annealing.

The Gaussian mixture model as it is presented here has the disadvantage that all eigenvectors of the local covariance matrix need to be extracted. However, this problem can be overcome if probabilistic PCA is used instead of standard PCA.

2.3.2   Mixture of probabilistic PCA

Tipping and Bishop (1999) extended the probabilistic PCA (section 2.1.2) to a mixture model. Different from the Gaussian mixture model, the probabilistic PCA extension needs only a set of $q < d$ principal components. The rest of the density's variance is given by the noise σ^2, which is the mean residual local variance. In the algorithm, the density (2.16) needs to be therefore replaced by the density used for probabilistic PCA. Apart from this substitution, the algorithm is identical to the classical Gaussian mixture model.

2.4   Kernel PCA

Different from the mixture models, kernel PCA (Schölkopf et al., 1998b) just works with a single PCA. It is an extension of PCA to non-linear distributions. Instead of directly doing a PCA, the n data points $\mathbf{x}_i$ are mapped into a higher-dimensional (possibly infinite-dimensional) feature space,

$$\mathbf{x}_i \rightarrow \varphi(\mathbf{x}_i) \ . \tag{2.22}$$

As it turns out later, the computation of this mapping can be omitted. In the feature space, principal components are extracted. That is, the following equation needs to be solved (here, we first assume that $\{\varphi(\mathbf{x}_i)\}$ has zero mean, see section 2.4.2):

$$\lambda \mathbf{w} = \mathbf{C} \mathbf{w} \ , \tag{2.23}$$

with the covariance matrix $\mathbf{C} = \frac{1}{n} \sum_{j=1}^{n} \varphi(\mathbf{x}_j) \varphi(\mathbf{x}_j)^T$. From the definition of $\mathbf{C}$ follows that $\mathbf{C}\mathbf{w}$ is a linear combination of the vectors $\varphi(\mathbf{x}_i)$. Thus, $\mathbf{w}$ must lie in the span of $\varphi(\mathbf{x}_1), \ldots, \varphi(\mathbf{x}_n)$. Hence, we can write

$$\mathbf{w} = \sum_{i=1}^{n} \alpha_i \varphi(\mathbf{x}_i) \ . \tag{2.24}$$

Combining (2.23) and (2.24) gives

$$\lambda \sum_{i=1}^{n} \alpha_i \varphi(\mathbf{x}_i) = \frac{1}{n} \sum_{i,j=1}^{n} \alpha_i \varphi(\mathbf{x}_j) \left(\varphi(\mathbf{x}_j)^T \varphi(\mathbf{x}_i) \right) \ , \tag{2.25}$$

which is equivalent to the set of n equations

$$\lambda \sum_{i=1}^{n} \alpha_i \left(\varphi(\mathbf{x}_i)^T \varphi(\mathbf{x}_l) \right) = \frac{1}{n} \sum_{i,j=1}^{n} \alpha_i \left(\varphi(\mathbf{x}_j)^T \varphi(\mathbf{x}_l) \right) \left(\varphi(\mathbf{x}_j)^T \varphi(\mathbf{x}_i) \right) \quad \forall\, l \,. \tag{2.26}$$

The direction from (2.26) to (2.25) is fulfilled because the left side of (2.25) is in the span of $\varphi(\mathbf{x}_1), \ldots, \varphi(\mathbf{x}_n)$, and (2.26) defines all n projections on $\varphi(\mathbf{x}_i)$. Equation (2.26) has the favorable property that it is written entirely with scalar products in the feature space. Hence, we do not need to carry out the transformation φ, which would be computationally impossible for an infinite-dimensional feature space. It is enough to work in the original space. Thus, instead of working with the scalar product $\varphi(\mathbf{x})^T \varphi(\mathbf{y})$, we are only working with a kernel function $k(\mathbf{x}, \mathbf{y}) = \varphi(\mathbf{x})^T \varphi(\mathbf{y})$. For the given data points, this function can be written as a matrix $\mathbf{K}$, with $K_{ij} = k(\mathbf{x}_i, \mathbf{x}_j)$. Using the kernel matrix, (2.26) can be written as

$$n\lambda \mathbf{K} \boldsymbol{\alpha} = \mathbf{K}^2 \boldsymbol{\alpha} \ , \tag{2.27}$$

with $\boldsymbol{\alpha} = (\alpha_1, \ldots, \alpha_n)^T$. As shown in appendix C.2, (2.27) is equivalent to

$$n\lambda \, \boldsymbol{\alpha} = \mathbf{K} \boldsymbol{\alpha} \ . \tag{2.28}$$

Thus, the vector $\boldsymbol{\alpha}$ for each principal component can be obtained by extracting the eigenvectors of $\mathbf{K}$. For further processing, the principal component $\mathbf{w}$ needs to be normalized to have unit length. This can be also established by working solely with the kernel,

$$\|\mathbf{w}\|^2 = \left(\sum_{i=1}^{n} \alpha_i \varphi(\mathbf{x}_i)\right)^T \left(\sum_{j=1}^{n} \alpha_j \varphi(\mathbf{x}_j)\right) = \boldsymbol{\alpha}^T \mathbf{K} \boldsymbol{\alpha} = n\lambda \boldsymbol{\alpha}^T \boldsymbol{\alpha} \ , \quad (2.29)$$

which results in a normalization rule for $\boldsymbol{\alpha}$.

To apply kernel PCA, a data point's features (the projections on the principal components) need to be extracted, and the formalism needs to be adjusted to distributions that do not have zero mean in feature space. These two points are addressed in the following sections. Furthermore, a short list of common kernel functions is given.

2.4.1   Feature extraction

The principal components are not directly accessible because $\varphi(\mathbf{x})$ is not known. However, projections onto the components can be computed (Schölkopf et al., 1998b). A projection f of a pattern $\mathbf{z}$ in the original space onto a principal component in feature space can be computed as follows:

$$f = \varphi(\mathbf{z})^T \mathbf{w} = \sum_{i=1}^{n} \alpha_i k(\mathbf{z}, \mathbf{x}_i) \ . \quad (2.30)$$

The computational load for each projection onto a principal component is high, n evaluations of $k(\mathbf{z}, \mathbf{x}_i)$ are needed. In appendix B.2, a speed-up is described that uses a reduced set of $m < n$ patterns, instead of $\{\mathbf{x}_i\}$. This reduces the computation time by the factor m/n (Schölkopf et al., 1998a).

2.4.2   Centering in feature space

So far, we have assumed that $\{\varphi(\mathbf{x}_i)\}$ has zero mean, which is usually not fulfilled. Therefore, the formalism needs to be adjusted (Schölkopf et al., 1998b). The following set of points will be centered:

$$\tilde{\varphi}(\mathbf{x}_i) = \varphi(\mathbf{x}_i) - \frac{1}{n} \sum_{r=1}^{n} \varphi(\mathbf{x}_r) \ . \quad (2.31)$$

The above analysis holds if the covariance matrix is computed from $\tilde{\varphi}(\mathbf{x}_i)$. Thus, the kernel matrix $K_{ij} = \varphi(\mathbf{x}_i)^T \varphi(\mathbf{x}_j)$ needs to be replaced by $\tilde{K}_{ij} = \tilde{\varphi}(\mathbf{x}_i)^T \tilde{\varphi}(\mathbf{x}_j)$. Using (2.31), $\tilde{K}$ can be written as,

$$\tilde{K}_{ij} = \varphi(\mathbf{x}_i)^T \varphi(\mathbf{x}_j) - \frac{1}{n} \sum_{r=1}^{n} \varphi(\mathbf{x}_i)^T \varphi(\mathbf{x}_r) - \frac{1}{n} \sum_{r=1}^{n} \varphi(\mathbf{x}_r)^T \varphi(\mathbf{x}_j)$$

$$+ \frac{1}{n^2} \sum_{r,s=1}^{n} \varphi(\mathbf{x}_r)^T \varphi(\mathbf{x}_s)$$

$$= K_{ij} - \frac{1}{n} \sum_{r=1}^{n} K_{ir} - \frac{1}{n} \sum_{r=1}^{n} K_{rj} + \frac{1}{n^2} \sum_{r,s=1}^{n} K_{rs} . \tag{2.32}$$

Therefore, we can evaluate the kernel matrix for the centered data using the known matrix $\mathbf{K}$. For the remainder of this thesis, I denote with $\boldsymbol{\alpha}$ the eigenvectors of $\tilde{\mathbf{K}}$ instead of $\mathbf{K}$, and they are normalized according to (2.29) using the eigenvalues of $\tilde{\mathbf{K}}$. The principal components are $\tilde{\mathbf{w}} = \sum_{i=1}^{n} \alpha_i \tilde{\varphi}(\mathbf{x}_i)$.

2.4.3 Common kernel functions

The kernel function needs to be a scalar product in some feature space. A sufficient condition is that the kernel matrix is positive semidefinite (Schölkopf et al., 1998b; Schölkopf and Smola, 2002, p. 44). Some common kernel functions that fulfill this condition are the polynomial kernel,

$$k(\mathbf{x}, \mathbf{y}) = (\mathbf{x}^T \mathbf{y})^d \tag{2.33}$$

with a constant integer d, the Gaussian kernel,

$$k(\mathbf{x}, \mathbf{y}) = \exp\left(-\frac{\|\mathbf{x} - \mathbf{y}\|^2}{2\sigma^2}\right) \tag{2.34}$$

with a constant $\sigma > 0$, and the inverse multiquadric kernel,

$$k(\mathbf{x}, \mathbf{y}) = \frac{1}{\sqrt{\|\mathbf{x} - \mathbf{y}\|^2 + c}} \tag{2.35}$$

with a constant $c > 0$ (Schölkopf and Smola, 2002, p. 54). The last two functions result in a kernel matrix with full rank (Micchelli, 1986). That is, all eigenvectors are linearly independent. Thus, the dimensionality of the feature space is not restricted (it is infinite).

Chapter 3

Mixture of local PCA

This chapter presents two new extensions to existing models to obtain a mixture of local PCA for modeling data distributions. The first section gives a motivation for using local PCA instead of code-book vectors or univariate densities. The following two sections present the two learning variants. The first variant is an extension of the vector quantizer Neural Gas (section 2.2.4) to local PCA. The second variant is a modification of the mixture of probabilistic PCA (section 2.3.2). The new variants were tested on synthetic data distributions and on a digit classification task. Finally, their advantages and disadvantages relative to each other are discussed. For the overall chapter, a training set consists of points $\mathbf{x}_i \in \mathbb{R}^d$ with $i = 1, \ldots, n$, and the mixture contains m units.

3.1 Motivation for local PCA

When describing a data distribution with a mixture model the question arises what kind of units should the mixture contain. The simplest local description is a point, the second simplest a linear model, which can be obtained from a local PCA. In a Gaussian density model of the data points, a point corresponds to a uniform Gaussian function, and a local PCA corresponds to a multivariate Gaussian (section 2.3.1). Thus, the local iso-density surface is a sphere respective an ellipsoid. Therefore, the decision between points and local PCA can be also regarded as a decision between spheres and ellipsoids. Despite its greater complexity, local PCA is favorable over a point for the following reasons. An ellipsoid can describe a local structure for which many spheres are needed (figure 3.1.A). Furthermore, sensorimotor distributions are usually constrained locally to subspaces with fewer dimensions than the space of the training data. Thus, directions exist in which locally the distribution has zero variance (or almost zero because of noise). PCA can omit directions of zero variance; a point cannot (figure 3.1.B). Using local PCA also helps to cope with the problem of noise dimensions as mentioned in section 1.5.5. An ellipsoid can extend with one of its principal components into the additional noise dimension; the number of points needed to take care of the additional variance increases over-proportionally (compare figure 3.1 with figure 1.9).

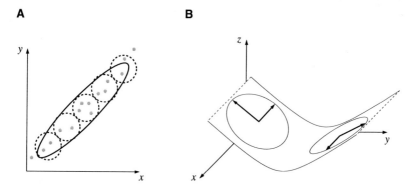

Figure 3.1: Advantage of ellipsoidal units opposed to spheres. A) An ellipse can describe a structure (gray dots) for which many circles are needed. B) The manifold surrounded by solid curves and dashed lines can be approximated by only two flat ellipsoids (thick arrows mark their principal axes).

3.2   Extension of Neural Gas to local PCA

The vector-quantization algorithm Neural Gas (section 2.2.4) is extended such that each code-book vector includes a local PCA (Hoffmann and Möller, 2003; Möller and Hoffmann, 2004). Henceforth, the new algorithm is called NGPCA. We chose Neural Gas because it results in a near homogeneous coverage of data distributions independent of the initial position of code-book vectors. First, NGPCA is described; then, a modification about the competition between units is presented. In the last part of this section, simulations demonstrate the operation of the algorithm.

3.2.1   Algorithm

In the extension of Neural Gas to NGPCA, a code-book vector is replaced by a hyper-ellipsoid. An ellipsoid has a center $\mathbf{c}_j$, and axes given by a local PCA, which extracts q eigenvectors $\mathbf{w}_j^l$ and eigenvalues λ_j^l with $l = 1, \ldots, q$. The size of the ellipsoid in the direction of the $d - q$ minor components is given by the mean residual variance σ_j^2 in these directions. The algorithm has the same annealing scheme as Neural Gas, and it also has the same parameters. Again, at the beginning of each annealing step, a data point is randomly drawn from the training set. After presenting a point $\mathbf{x}$ the centers $\mathbf{c}_j$ are updated as the code-book vectors in Neural Gas,

$$\mathbf{c}_j(t+1) = \mathbf{c}_j(t) + \alpha_j \cdot [\mathbf{x} - \mathbf{c}_j(t)] \quad . \tag{3.1}$$

The weight α_j is defined by $\alpha_j = \varepsilon \cdot \exp(-r_j/\varrho)$. The learning rate ε and the neighborhood range ϱ decrease exponentially during training. r_j is again the rank of the unit j with respect to $\mathbf{x}$. In the following, the unit index j is omitted for simplicity. All equations need to be evaluated for each unit separately.

The ranking of the units cannot depend on the Euclidean distance anymore, since this would ignore the shape of the ellipsoids. Instead, an elliptical error measure is chosen,

$$E(\mathbf{x}) = \boldsymbol{\xi}^T \mathbf{W} \boldsymbol{\Lambda}^{-1} \mathbf{W}^T \boldsymbol{\xi} + \frac{1}{\sigma^2} \left(\boldsymbol{\xi}^T \boldsymbol{\xi} - \boldsymbol{\xi}^T \mathbf{W} \mathbf{W}^T \boldsymbol{\xi} \right) + \ln \det \boldsymbol{\Lambda} + (d - q) \ln \sigma^2 . \tag{3.2}$$

This measure is a normalized Mahalanobis distance plus reconstruction error (Hinton et al., 1997). $\boldsymbol{\xi} = \mathbf{x} - \mathbf{c}$ is the deviation of the vector $\mathbf{x}$ from the center of a unit. The matrix $\mathbf{W}$ contains in its columns the eigenvectors $\mathbf{w}^l$, and the diagonal matrix $\boldsymbol{\Lambda}$ contains the eigenvalues λ^l. It can be shown (appendix C.1) that this error measure is the same (up to a constant) as the double negative logarithm of the local probability density given in probabilistic PCA. Thus, a unit can be interpreted as a local density $p(\mathbf{x}) = (2\pi)^{-d/2} \exp(-E(\mathbf{x})/2)$, and the units are ranked in the order of the probabilities of $\mathbf{x}$ originating from the single units. However, the computation of the probability is not necessary since the same result is obtained by ordering the units using the error $E(\mathbf{x})$. The unit resulting in the smallest $E(\mathbf{x})$ has rank zero, and the one with the largest $E(\mathbf{x})$ has rank $m - 1$.

The second term in (3.2) is the reconstruction error divided by σ^2. σ depends on the estimate of the total residual variance v_{res}, which is updated according to

$$v_{\text{res}}(t+1) = v_{\text{res}}(t) + \alpha \cdot \left(\boldsymbol{\xi}^T \boldsymbol{\xi} - \boldsymbol{\xi}^T \mathbf{W} \mathbf{W}^T \boldsymbol{\xi} - v_{\text{res}}(t) \right) \quad . \tag{3.3}$$

The total residual variance is evenly distributed among all $d - q$ minor dimensions by

$$\sigma^2 = \frac{v_{\text{res}}}{d - q} \quad . \tag{3.4}$$

This equation is the same as for the noise in probabilistic PCA (2.11). To adjust the principal axes and their lengths, we do one step with an on-line PCA method:

$$\{\mathbf{W}(t+1), \mathbf{\Lambda}(t+1)\} = \text{PCA}\{\mathbf{W}(t), \mathbf{\Lambda}(t), \boldsymbol{\xi}(t), \alpha(t)\} \ . \tag{3.5}$$

We use a PCA algorithm similar to the robust recursive least square algorithm (RRLSA) (Ouyang et al., 2000). RRLSA is a sequential network of single-neuron principal component analyzers based on deflation of the input vector (Sanger, 1989). While the $\mathbf{w}^l$ are normalized to unit length, internally the algorithm works with unnormalized $\tilde{\mathbf{w}}^l$, which are updated according to

$$\tilde{\mathbf{w}}^l(t+1) = \tilde{\mathbf{w}}^l(t) + \alpha \cdot \left(\boldsymbol{\xi}^{(l)} y_l - \tilde{\mathbf{w}}^l(t) \right), \quad \text{for } l = 1, \ldots, q \ . \tag{3.6}$$

y_l is a component of the vector $\mathbf{y} = \mathbf{W}^T \boldsymbol{\xi}$. The deflated vector $\boldsymbol{\xi}^{(l)}$ is computed by iterating

$$\boldsymbol{\xi}^{(l+1)} = \boldsymbol{\xi}^{(l)} - \mathbf{w}^l y_l \quad \text{starting with} \quad \boldsymbol{\xi}^{(1)} = \boldsymbol{\xi} \ . \tag{3.7}$$

After each step t, the eigenvalue and eigenvector estimates are obtained from

$$\lambda^l = \|\tilde{\mathbf{w}}^l\|, \quad \mathbf{w}^l = \frac{\tilde{\mathbf{w}}^l}{\|\tilde{\mathbf{w}}^l\|}, \quad \text{for } l = 1, \ldots, q \ . \tag{3.8}$$

Since the orthogonality of $\mathbf{W}$ is not fully preserved for each step, the algorithm has to be combined with an orthogonalization method, here we used Gram-Schmidt (Möller, 2002). Orthogonality is essential for the computation of the error (3.2). This orthogonalization concludes one annealing step.

The unit centers are initialized by randomly chosen examples from the training set. The eigenvector estimates are initialized with random orthogonal vectors. The eigenvalues λ_j^l and the variances σ_j^2 are initially set to one. To avoid zero variance in a direction during the computation of the local PCA, a uniform noise randomly chosen from the interval $[-0.0005; 0.0005]$ is added to each component of a randomly drawn data point (for all experiments).

3.2.2   Alternative distance measure

For some applications, it proved to be of advantage to modify the error measure $E(\mathbf{x})$. The error (3.2) depends on the size of the hyper-ellipsoid. Its volume is proportional to $V = \sqrt{\det \mathbf{\Lambda}} \, \sigma^{d-q}$. For a big ellipsoid, (3.2) has therefore a huge bias, namely $2 \ln V$. Thus, if the other ellipsoids are much smaller, this huge ellipsoid often has a high rank, independent of the

Euclidean distance of $\mathbf{x}$ to the center of the ellipsoid. Since the weight α decreases exponentially with the rank, α is almost zero, and the ellipsoid cannot change its size anymore, it is 'dead' (for example, figure 3.8.A). Thus, to avoid dead units, we tested an alternative error measure that is independent of the volume of the ellipsoid. This can be achieved by normalizing λ^l and σ such that the resulting volume $\tilde{V}$ is one. Let $\tilde{\lambda}^l$ and $\tilde{\sigma}$ be the normalized values. They can be computed by

$$\tilde{\lambda}^l = \frac{\lambda^l}{\sqrt[d]{V^2}}$$

$$\tilde{\sigma} = \frac{\sigma}{\sqrt[d]{V}} \ . \tag{3.9}$$

Using these substitutions, it can be straight-forwardly verified that the new volume $\tilde{V} = \tilde{\sigma}^{d-q} \prod_{l=1}^{q} \tilde{\lambda}^{l/2}$ fulfills $\tilde{V} = 1$. To compute the modified error, we replace λ^l and σ by their normalized values, and then we use the substitution (3.9) to obtain the error again in the original variables,

$$\tilde{E}(\mathbf{x}) = \left(\boldsymbol{\xi}^T \mathbf{W} \boldsymbol{\Lambda}^{-1} \mathbf{W}^T \boldsymbol{\xi} + \frac{1}{\sigma^2} \left(\boldsymbol{\xi}^T \boldsymbol{\xi} - \boldsymbol{\xi}^T \mathbf{W} \mathbf{W}^T \boldsymbol{\xi} \right) \right) V^{2/d} \ . \tag{3.10}$$

Here, the logarithm terms can be omitted because they are the same for all units. The modified algorithm uses (3.10) instead of (3.2) for the competition of the units. Everything else stays unchanged. The ellipsoids are still allowed to change their size according to the local PCA. In the following, this algorithm will be called 'NGPCA-constV', in contrast to NGPCA, which uses (3.2) for the competition.

3.2.3 Simulations

The operation of the algorithm is demonstrated on two synthetic ring-ling-square distributions. The data points in these distributions are uniformly distributed over the area of a ring, a line, and a square. The outer radius of the ring equals 1.0. The first variant consists of 850 data points (figure 3.2); the second is much more sparse and contains only 85 points (figure 3.3).

In this section, all tests used the same parameters. Ten units were used. For each, two principal components were extracted. The further training parameter settings were $\varrho(0) = 1.0$, $\varrho(t_{\max}) = 0.001$, $\varepsilon(0) = 0.5$, $\varepsilon(t_{\max}) = 0.001$, and $t_{\max} = 30\,000$. The quality of a fitted mixture model was evaluated by computing log-likelihoods. As mentioned before, each unit can be interpreted as a local probability density, $p(\mathbf{x}|j) = (2\pi)^{-d/2} \exp(-E_j(\mathbf{x})/2)$

(appendix C.1). These local densities allow the definition of a total density underlying the data distribution. It remains to define the priors, the weights of the local units. The prior $P(j)$ is set equal to the fraction of data points assigned to unit j. This assignment is obtained using hard-clustering based on (3.2). Given the priors, the log-likelihood per pattern is

$$\mathcal{L} = \frac{1}{n} \sum_{i=1}^{n} \ln \sum_{j=1}^{m} P(j)p(\mathbf{x}_i|j) \ . \tag{3.11}$$

To compute $p(\mathbf{x}|j)$, NGPCA-constV uses (3.2) for $E_j(\mathbf{x})$ and (3.10) to obtain the prior $P(j)$, since the modification just affects the competition between units.

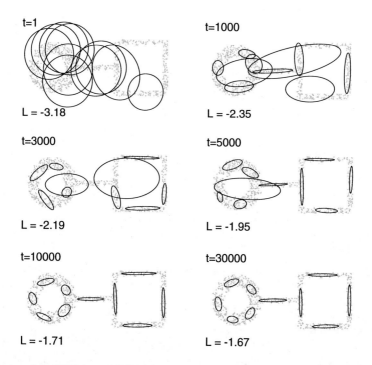

Figure 3.2: Training of NGPCA, shown at different annealing steps t. For each step, the log-likelihood per pattern $\mathcal{L}$ is shown. The length of each ellipse semi-axis is $\sqrt{\lambda_j^l}$.

The first test, using NGPCA, shows the incremental adjustment of the ellipses to the ring-line-square distribution with 850 points (figure 3.2). Here, only one training cycle is shown, but the performance was stable over different training cycles. In ten cycles, the final fitted model resembled the one shown in figure 3.2, and the final $\mathcal{L}$ ranged between -1.669 and -1.665. NGPCA-constV resulted in similar fitted models; here, the final $\mathcal{L}$ ranged between -1.688 and -1.668. However, the time evolution was a bit different: single large ellipses as in figure 3.2 (for t = 1000, 3000, and 5000) did not appear. Instead, the sizes of the ellipses were more balanced. Further examples can be found in Möller and Hoffmann (2004) and in section 3.3.2.

The second test compared NGPCA with NGPCA-constV by using the sparse distribution. Here, NGPCA-constV visibly outperformed NGPCA (figure 3.3). The results shown were typical.

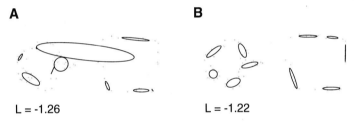

A   **B**

L = -1.26   L = -1.22

Figure 3.3: Results for the final fitted model using (A) NGPCA and (B) NGPCA-constV.

3.3 Extension of the mixture of probabilistic PCA

As an alternative to the presented extension of Neural Gas to local PCA, a modified version of the mixture of probabilistic PCA (Tipping and Bishop, 1999) was used. In the following, the modifications are described and motivated. Then, the obtained algorithm is tested on synthetic pattern sets.

3.3.1 Algorithm

The mixture of probabilistic PCA is also composed of m local PCA units, which have a center $\mathbf{c}_j$, eigenvectors $\mathbf{w}_j^l$, eigenvalues λ_j^l, and a residual variance σ_j^2. In the beginning, the centers are initialized with a vector quantizer. Then, the likelihood is maximized using an expectation-maximization iteration (section 2.3.1). As it is common to all Gaussian mixture models without annealing, this iteration may get stuck in a local optimum. Therefore, a proper initialization of the centers is important. However, this initialization is not mentioned in Tipping and Bishop (1999). Thus, the first important modification is to use Neural Gas to obtain the initial position of the centers. For Neural Gas, the standard parameter set was $\varrho(0) = 0.1m$, $\varrho(t_{\max}) = 0.0001$, $\varepsilon(0) = 0.5$, $\varepsilon(t_{\max}) = 0.05$, and $t_{\max} = 3000\,m$ (for all of this thesis except of section 3.3.2).

The algorithm iterates an expectation and a maximization step. In the expectation step, the posterior probabilities are computed (section 2.3.1). In the maximization step, the eigenvectors, the eigenvalues, and the residual variance of the units are computed. Here, different from Tipping and Bishop (1999), RRLSA as described in section 3.2.1 is used to compute the eigenvectors and eigenvalues. For all experiments in this thesis except the tests in section 3.3.2, in total, 40 expectation and 40 maximization steps were iterated.

During each maximization step, the algorithm goes through a fixed number of RRLSA steps (30 times the number of training patterns). For each of these steps, a pattern is drawn from the set $\{\mathbf{x}_i\}$. Then, given the pattern $\mathbf{x}_i$, a unit j is randomly chosen depending on its posterior probability $P(j|\mathbf{x}_i)$. For this unit the eigenvectors and eigenvalues are updated using (3.6), (3.7), and (3.8), as before.

The learning rate α_j in RRLSA is computed for each unit separately. Let t_j be the number of times the unit j was chosen. At the beginning of each maximization step, t_j restarts from zero. With increasing t_j, the learning rate decays as $\alpha_j = 1/t_j$. This decay rule guarantees that the result for each unit converges to an average over the presented patterns (appendix A.3).

After the eigenvectors and eigenvalues are computed, also the residual variance σ_j^2 is obtained recursively. Here, the update equations are also the same as the ones used in NGPCA, namely (3.3) and (3.4). The learning rate α_j is computed as above. The principal components were extracted before computing σ_j^2 because (3.3) relies on orthonormal vectors $\mathbf{w}_j^l$. At the beginning of the algorithm, the entries of $\mathbf{W}$ were set to random values, and then, $\mathbf{W}$ was made orthonormal. The eigenvalues and the residual variance were initially set to one.

Using an on-line algorithm like RRLSA is of advantage since for each randomly drawn pattern, random noise can be added. If a unit has in its neighborhood only a few patterns the variance in some directions will be zero. Thus, the PCA yields eigenvalues with zero value. Computationally, such eigenvalues are a problem because the corresponding probability density has an infinite peak. With the addition of noise, however, zero variance can be avoided. In the original algorithm suggested by Tipping and Bishop (1999), the computation of the eigenvectors and eigenvalues is done by one step in batch mode. Here, the variance of single points cannot be increased by adding noise. For all experiments, the added noise for each dimension was in the interval $[-0.005; 0.005]$.

The last modification is a correction for 'empty' units, these are units with a prior $P(j) < 1/n$. Such empty units can either result from the Neural Gas initialization (Daszykowski et al., 2002), or they can occur during the expectation-maximization iteration. In the correction, the center of the empty unit is moved near to the center of the unit with the largest prior (within a random deviation from the interval [-0.01;0.01] in the direction of the principal component). The eigenvectors, the eigenvalues, and the residual variance of the empty unit are set equal to the ones of the largest unit. Then, both units re-adjust their prior and posterior probabilities to one half the values of the former largest unit. Thus, the ellipsoids of both units overlap. The slight deviation of the centers will eventually lead to the separation of the ellipsoids in further steps of the expectation-maximization iteration (section 3.3.2). In the following, the original mixture of probabilistic PCA will be called 'MPPCA', and the presented extension 'MPPCA-ext'.

3.3.2 Simulations

The simulations show the operation of MPPCA-ext on synthetic distributions. The examples demonstrate the importance of the initialization, the occurrence of empty units, and that the algorithm can separate overlapping ellipses. Finally, some tests compare MPPCA-ext with NGPCA. As in section 3.2.3 the ring-line-square sets with 850 points and with 85 points were used. Further pattern sets are a three-dimensional spiral distribution and a two-dimensional two-lines distribution. The spiral is composed of 1000 points, its radius is 1.2, and its length is 5.0. The points were uniformly distributed along the spiral, which had a thickness of 0.02. The two-lines distribution contained two slightly tilted lines (length: 5.1, thickness: 0.2), each of them consisted of 50 points.

The number of units used was ten for all distributions but two-lines, for which two units were used. For all tests, two principal components were extracted. Both Neural Gas for the initialization and NGPCA used the same parameter set as in section 3.2.3. For MPPCA-ext, the number of expectation and maximization steps is either given or the algorithm iterates until convergence. In all tests, the log-likelihood per pattern $\mathcal{L}$ was evaluated (see section 3.2.3).

Using the ring-line-square distribution with 850 points, the first test shows the importance of a good initialization. Here, the other modifications did not matter. Figure 3.4 shows that the initialization of the center positions with k-means may lead to undesired local maxima. On the other hand, the

Neural Gas initialization reliably resulted in good model fits (figure 3.5). Over ten separate training cycles, the log-likelihood ranged between -1.663 and -1.653. Figure 3.5 further demonstrates how the ellipses move to fit the distribution better.

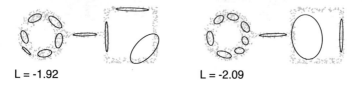

L = -1.92   L = -2.09

Figure 3.4: MPPCA converged to a local maximum after starting with k-means. Results from two random initializations of k-means are shown. For each result, the log-likelihood per pattern $\mathcal{L}$ is shown. The length of each ellipse semi-axis is $\sqrt{\lambda_j^l}$.

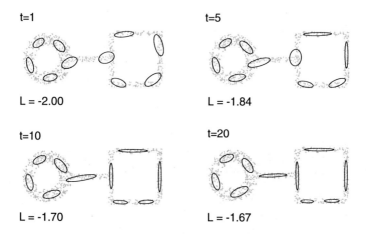

t=1   t=5

L = -2.00   L = -1.84

t=10   t=20

L = -1.70   L = -1.67

Figure 3.5: Training of MPPCA-ext, shown at different EM steps t. For each step, the log-likelihood per pattern $\mathcal{L}$ is shown.

The second test on the same distribution demonstrates that the ellipses can spread meaningful over the distribution after they all overlap at the beginning (figure 3.6)[1]. A PCA extracted the two eigenvectors and the corresponding eigenvalues of the covariance matrix of the pattern set. All ten

---

[1]Here, MPPCA behaves the same as MPPCA-ext, since the extensions do not matter.

units started with these eigenvectors and eigenvalues; their centers were distributed around the center of the distribution, with random deviations along the principal component. Prior and posterior probabilities were initially the same for all units. Here, the initialization with a single PCA led to a good model fit. However, this does not work for all distributions; therefore, Neural Gas was used instead. Neural Gas also results in a faster convergence (compare the t values between figure 3.5 and figure 3.6).

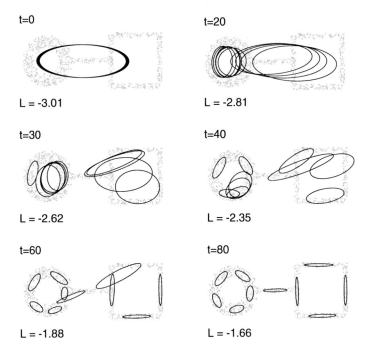

Figure 3.6: Training of MPPCA after initializing all ten units with a single PCA.

Using the sparse ring-line-square set (85 points), the third test shows the occurrence of an empty unit and the consequences of the following correction. Empty units were only observed for sparse distributions. Figure 3.7 illustrates the removal and reappearance of an empty unit. This figure and figure 3.3 already show a comparison between MPPCA-ext, NGPCA, and NGPCA-constV. Before the empty unit correction, the fitted models of MPPCA-ext and NGPCA-constV resembled each other.

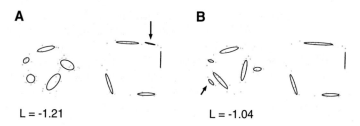

Figure 3.7: MPPCA-ext with empty unit correction: (A) after one EM step, the arrow points to the unit that is going to vanish, (B) after convergence, the arrow points to the area where the empty unit reappeared.

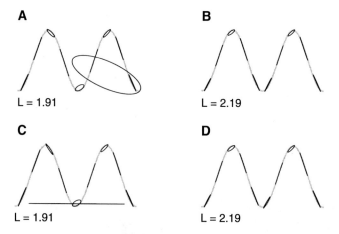

Figure 3.8: Three-dimensional spiral distribution. (A) NGPCA ends up with a dead ellipsoid. (B) NGPCA with ten times as many annealing steps avoids the dead ellipsoid. (C) NGPCA-constV with the same parameters as in B produces a long ellipsoid connecting distant parts of the spiral. (D) MPPCA-ext results in about the same fitted model as for NGPCA in B.

The thin spiral and the two-lines distributions were used for more comparisons between the different algorithms. Figure 3.8.A shows that NGPCA ends up with a dead ellipsoid on the thin spiral. However, the dead ellipsoid can be avoided if the annealing is slower ($t_{\mathrm{max}} = 300\,000$) (figure 3.8.B). In contrast, NGPCA-constV for slow and fast annealing produces an undesired long ellipsoid that stretches to distant parts of the distribution (figure 3.8.C). Like the slow NGPCA, MPPCA-ext produces a good fitted model (figure

3.8.D). The next test shows an example on which MPPCA-ext failed. Using the two-lines distribution, the expectation-maximization iteration ends in an inappropriate local maximum because the Neural Gas initialization cannot distinguish between the two lines (figure 3.9.A). In contrast, both NGPCA variants can cope with the two-lines distribution (figure 3.9.B).

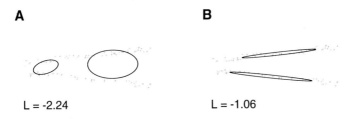

A

B

L = -2.24

L = -1.06

Figure 3.9: The final fitted model is shown for (A) MPPCA-ext and (B) NGPCA.

3.4 Digit classification

The classification of hand-written digits was used as a high-dimensional test for the new mixtures of local PCA models. The performance is comparable to other methods from the literature. Moreover, both NGPCA and NGPCA-constV are better then Neural Gas and PCA alone.

3.4.1 Methods

The digits were taken from the MNIST database (LeCun, 1998), which is a subset of the NIST database produced by the U.S. National Institute of Standards and Technology (appendix D). The database contains 60 000 images of digits for training and 10 000 for testing. The gray-scale images (scaled to pixel values in the interval $[0, 1]$) are centered in a 28×28 pixel grid.

Two training sets were generated (Möller and Hoffmann, 2004). One contained the original 28×28 images transformed into 784 dimensional vectors. The other one was composed of subsampled images of size 8×8 transformed into 64 dimensional vectors. The subsampled images were obtained by removing a margin of 4 pixels, such that the digits in the resulting 20×20 image fitted tightly into the frame. Each of the pixels of the final 8×8 image was produced by a weighted summation over a local region, using a Gaussian weight function with a half-width of 1.25 pixels (in the 20×20 image).

This second training set used only the first 1000 images of each digit[2]. Each training set was split into ten parts, one part for each digit.

Each digit was trained by one model, separately. The local PCA mixture models contained ten units with ten principal components. Both NG-PCA and NGPCA-constV used the parameter set: $t_{max} = 30\,000$, $\varrho(0) = 2$, $\varrho(t_{max}) = 0.002$, $\varepsilon(0) = 0.5$, $\varepsilon(t_{max}) = 0.0002$.

The results for the 28×28 training set were compared to a single PCA, which extracted 40 principal components for each digit. The single PCA had fewer parameters then the mixture model because higher numbers of principal components did not improve the classification (using more components makes the ellipsoids thicker, thus ellipsoids from different digits probably overlapp). Moreover, the results were compared to standard Neural Gas, which contained 109 code-book vectors (as many as required to obtain about the same number of free parameters as for the local PCA mixture). Neural Gas used the same training parameters as NGPCA.

To classify a digit, the error measure (3.2) was computed for all units of the ten fitted models, and the digit was assigned to the model that comprised the unit with the minimal error value. In the standard Neural Gas case, the Euclidean distance was used instead of (3.2).

3.4.2 Results

The results for the classification of the 28×28 digits are shown in table 3.1. The error rates for the two NGPCA variants were averaged over three separate training cycles (the difference between best and worst was around 0.2% for both variants). Both variants are better then a model using only a single PCA, and also better then Neural Gas with the same number of free parameters. MPPCA-ext could not be tested on this set because the large distances between digits lead to numerical zero probabilities (the maximum distance in a 784-dimensional cube of side length one is 28, this is large compared to a σ of around 0.1).

In the following, the ellipsoids of the NGPCA model are visualized (Möller and Hoffmann, 2004). Figure 3.10 shows the centers of the ten ellipsoids for each digit. Each center represents the local average over a subgroup of digits. Different ways to write a digit become visible, for example, digit '7' with or without a cross-bar.

The ellipsoid axis (eigenvectors) for one digit are visualized in figure 3.11. The eigenvectors represent variations around a center. This can be illustrated by adding multiples of an eigenvector to a center (figure 3.12). In the

---

[2]The number of training patterns is different in Möller and Hoffmann (2004), where in total 60 000 patterns were used for the 8×8 image set.

training method	error
NGPCA	2.79%
NGPCA-constV	2.77%
PCA	4.85%
Neural Gas	4.22%

Table 3.1: Classification performance on digits of size 28 × 28 from a training set composed of 60000 digits. The extension of Neural Gas to local PCA (NGPCA) is compared to PCA and Neural Gas.

Figure 3.10: Centers of all units obtained from NGPCA.

presented example, different sizes of the digit '2' are covered by the local PCA.

Figure 3.13 shows a sample of mis-classified digits. Some of the mis-classified digits resemble the center they were assigned to (for example, the digit '9'). These digits seem to be extremes that lie close to representatives of another class.

Figure 3.11: Center (left image) and eigenvectors (from left to right in the order of the descending eigenvalues) of one unit of the fitted model for the digit '2'. In the eigenvector diagrams, white and black indicate positive respective negative components.

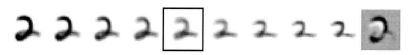

Figure 3.12: Variation of a digit by adding multiples of the principal eigenvector $\mathbf{w}^1$ to the center $\mathbf{c}$. The center image $\mathbf{c}$ is marked by a frame, the eigenvector $\mathbf{w}^1$ is shown on the right side. From the center to the left, $-0.5\sqrt{\lambda^1}\mathbf{w}^1$ is added to each picture. Thus, the picture on the very left deviates by $-2\sqrt{\lambda^1}\mathbf{w}^1$ from the center. From the center image to the right, the vector $0.5\sqrt{\lambda^1}\mathbf{w}^1$ is added. The principal eigenvalue was $\lambda^1 = 5.2$.

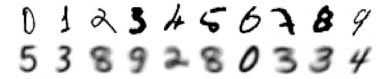

Figure 3.13: Sample of the mis-classified digits. The first mis-classified digit of each class is shown (top row, class '0' to '9' from left to right) together with the center vector of the unit to which the pattern was assigned (bottom row).

The training set with digits of size 8×8 was used for a comparison with MPPCA-ext, and also for a comparison with local PCA mixture models from the literature (Hinton et al., 1997; Tipping and Bishop, 1999). These models worked on a different data set (CEDAR, which is commercial), however the size of the images (8×8) and the number of training patterns (1000 per digit) were the same. Moreover, these models had the same complexity as our models, namely ten units with ten principal components each. Tipping and Bishop (1999) used the discussed MPPCA model, and Hinton et al. (1997) used a mixture model that minimized the reconstruction error (as mentioned in section 2.3). Other mixture models that were tested on hand-written digits have a different complexity, for example, Meinicke and Ritter (2001) used a variable number of principal components. These models were excluded because they are hard to compare. Table 3.2 shows the result of the comparison. The errors from our models were averaged over three separate training cycles (the difference between worst and best was around 0.2%). Tipping and Bishop (1999) presented the result of the best training cycle.

training method	database	error
NGPCA	MNIST	4.78%
NGPCA-constV	MNIST	4.64%
MPPCA-ext	MNIST	4.58%
Tipping and Bishop (1999)	CEDAR	4.64%
Hinton et al. (1997)	CEDAR	4.91%

Table 3.2: Classification performance on digits of size 8×8 from a training set composed of 10000 digits. Results are compared to two other local PCA mixture models that have the same complexity.

3.5 Discussion

Two local PCA mixture models were presented. The first model is an extension of Neural Gas to local PCA. The code-book vectors of Neural Gas are replaced by local PCA units. Two different variants were shown. One (NGPCA) uses the normalized Mahalanobis distance plus reconstruction error for the competition between units. The other one (NGPCA-constV) uses a modified error measure that ignores the volume of the ellipsoid associated with the local PCA.

The second model is an extension of the mixture of probabilistic PCA (MPPCA-ext). It contains three modifications: first, an initialization with Neural Gas; second, a neural network (RRLSA) to extract the local principal components, this network allows the addition of noise for each on-line presentation of a training pattern; third, a correction for units that have no patterns assigned to them.

Both models could successfully fit synthetic two- and three-dimensional training data, and they could be used to classify hand-written digits. No clear advantage of one model over the other could be observed. Both have advantages and disadvantages relative to each other.

NGPCA and NGPCA-constV worked on data with arbitrarily many dimensions; MPPCA-ext failed on the 784-dimensional data because of numerical instabilities. Furthermore, data distributions can be constructed (the two-lines distribution, figure 3.9) on which MPPCA-ext ends in a local optimum, but both NGPCA variants find the global optimum. Different from the Neural Gas initialization in MPPCA-ext, NGPCA considers the shape of the ellipses during annealing, and can therefore fit them to the distribution before the annealing cools down and gets trapped in a local optimum. However, the two-lines distribution is highly artificial, a sensorimotor distribution likely does not comprise two parallel or almost parallel planes that are also close to each other.

On the other hand, MPPCA-ext is less sensitive to the Neural Gas parameters (t_{max}, $\rho(0)$, $\rho(t_{max})$, $\varepsilon(0)$, and $\varepsilon(t_{max})$); for some distributions (especially the visuomotor model discussed in chapter 6), NGPCA depends on these parameters. For MPPCA-ext, standard parameters could be defined that worked for all tests in this thesis. Further, MPPCA-ext is mathematically more sound. It maximizes the likelihood of the data given an assumption on the density; NGPCA is heuristic. We could not prove that NGPCA optimizes any specific function. However, it seems to maximize the likelihood as well.

A disadvantage of NGPCA is that it may produce dead units that do not get updated anymore (figure 3.8.A). To avoid dead units, the variant NGPCA-const was introduced, which worked better on sparsely distributed data (figure 3.3). On the thin spiral distribution, however, NGPCA-constV resulted in a thin ellipsoid that protruded out of the spiral and connected distant parts (figure 3.8.C). This result occurred probably because here the normalization of the ellipsoid's volume had the opposite effect to the case of a huge ellipsoid; for ellipsoids with a tiny volume, the NGPCA error measure (3.2) results in a low weight α, but the NGPCA-const error measure (3.10) is independent of the volume. Thus, for NGPCA-constV, chances are higher that patterns are assigned to the thin ellipsoid. For all NGPCA variants, these chances are highest in the direction of the ellipsoid's tips. Therefore, NGPCA-constV might attract distant patterns in these directions.

In this chapter, the advantages of just two of the three modification of MPPCA were visible. The good fit of the ring-line-square data and probably also the slight improvement of the digit classification result from the new Neural Gas initialization. For the tasks in this thesis, this initialization seemed to cure most problems with local optima associated with MPPCA. Therefore, MPPCA was preferred over those approaches that include annealing into the EM-iteration (Meinicke and Ritter, 2001; Albrecht et al., 2000) because they also include many training parameters. The second modification, the correction for empty units was helpful to fit sparse data distributions (figure 3.7). The advantage of the third modification, adding noise to increase the variance of each training pattern, was not shown, but it proved to be necessary for approximating sensorimotor distributions (chapter 6).

The new extension of Neural Gas to local PCA is clearly better on the digit classification then Neural Gas (with the same number of free parameters) and PCA alone. Despite the apparent complexity of the task, a single linear model describes each digit quite well (resulting in 4.85% miss-classified digits). Thus, digit-classification does not seem to be an ideal test for a local PCA mixture model, though it is a popular test (Hinton et al., 1997; Tipping and Bishop, 1999; Meinicke and Ritter, 2001). Moreover, no PCA mixture model can compete with neural networks specifically designed for hand-written-digit classification. The best of these models has an error of 0.67% (LeCun et al., 1998). The performance difference in the classification for the different training sets with images of size 28×28 and 8×8 (2.79% compared to 4.78% for NGPCA) results in a large part from the different numbers of training patterns. With the same number of patterns as for the 28×28 case, NGPCA has an error rate of 3.11% on the 8×8 images (Möller and Hoffmann, 2004).

The similarity of NGPCA and MPPCA provides a common bases for a mixture of ellipsoids, upon which a pattern recall as described in the following chapter can take place. If we ignore the priors then the resulting fitted models can be described by the same variables: $\mathbf{c}_j$, $\mathbf{W}_j$, $\mathbf{\Lambda}_j$, and σ_j. In addition, both methods provide the same error function (3.2) for each unit defined on these variables. The minimum of this error function over all units is an estimate for the squared distance to the distribution of training patterns. This estimate will be the basis for the pattern recall.

Chapter 4

Abstract recurrent neural networks

A pattern-association method is described that is based on a mixture of local PCA, which approximates a data distribution (chapter 3). We call the pattern association together with the approximation of the data distribution an abstract recurrent neural network. Analogue to a recall in a recurrent neural network, input and output components can be chosen arbitrarily after training. The output is said to be associated with the input. In the new model, the input is the offset of a constrained space whose span is the output space. The intersection of the constrained space with the mixture of ellipsoids gives the completed pattern. The algorithm was applied to function approximation, image completion, and the kinematics of a redundant robot arm in simulation. In the latter, a trained abstract recurrent neural network could be used both for the forward and the inverse kinematics. Experiments showed that the recall error increased with the number of input dimensions for a given trained network. To explain this increase, a simplified stochastic version of the mixture of local PCA is analyzed.

4.1 Motivation

First, favorable properties of recurrent neural networks (RNN) are mentioned, and reasons are given for using an abstract RNN that is based on the statistics of the training data rather than a network of neurons. Second, this section illustrates that a pattern completion might end in a local minimum if the completion is realized as a gradient descent in a potential field build on top of a mixture model. Thus, a different strategy is required.

4.1.1 Why abstract recurrent neural networks?

Recurrent neural networks have two main advantages over feed-forward networks (Movellan and McClelland, 1993; Steinkühler and Cruse, 1998): first, they do not fail on tasks that provide many possible solutions for a given input since RNNs relaxe to one possible solution. Second, the role of input and output neurons can be chosen after training. Thus, the same sensorimotor network can, for example, be used as a forward model and as an inverse model.

Evidently, RNNs exist in the brain (see, for example, Nakazawa et al. (2002)). So far, however, computational RNNs that are able to learn sensorimotor relationships are missing. Existing models either cannot be trained (Steinkühler and Cruse, 1998; Cruse, 2001), or cannot be used for arbitrary functional relationships (Hopfield, 1982, 1984). Although recurrent connections are widespread in biological nervous systems, their specific functions and the corresponding learning mechanisms are still widely unknown, and thus do not offer a direct approach to this problem. Moreover, since we did not see how to construct a computational recurrent network that can also learn to approximate functions, we developed an abstract network with the desired characteristics. This step was further motivated by potential field models (Bachmann et al., 1987; Dembo and Zeitouni, 1988). They can store arbitrarily many patterns, which are the minima of a potential field. In recall, these models descent into the minima. However, they do not generalize; the data are just stored.

4.1.2   Potential fields and local minima

For the mixture model, to obtain a potential field, the following two possibilities exist (they are not exclusive): use the negative of the probability density function (the sum of Gaussian functions), or use the sum of inverse Mahalanobis distances over all units (equivalent to a sum over Coulomb potentials (Bachmann et al., 1987)).

Given a potential field, a functional mapping from an input to an output can be achieved by defining a constrained subspace whose offset from zero is given by the input. Then, the completion of the input, which yields the output in its components, can be gained by finding a point on the constraint that has a minimal potential value. A gradient descent along the constraint may be used to find this minimum.

However, this gradient descent may end in a local minimum (figure 4.1). For both the negative density and the inverse-Mahalanobis potential, a potential valley corresponding to an ellipsoid may extend along the tips of the ellipsoid toward the constraint. At the intersection, this valley results in a local minimum within the constrained space. Such a local minimum may be far away from the distribution of training patterns and must therefore be avoided. Thus, instead of computing a gradient descent in a potential field, we directly compute the point on the constraint that is closest to the closest ellipsoid.

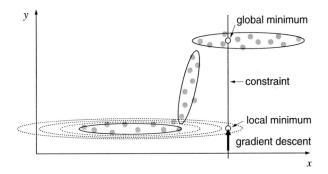

Figure 4.1: A constrained gradient descent (thick arrow) in a potential field constructed on top of the ellipses is likely to end in local minimum. Ellipses are iso-potential curves of a local field. The dotted curves illustrate a valley in the potential field.

4.2 Recall algorithm

The goal of the recall is to complete a pattern $\mathbf{p}$ whose components are only partially given (Hoffmann and Möller, 2003). The resulting pattern $\mathbf{z}$ shares the components of $\mathbf{p}$ that are defined as input.

After learning, the data distribution is represented by a collection of hyper-ellipsoids; each has a center $\mathbf{c}_j$, direction vectors $\mathbf{w}_j^l$ (principal axes), semi-axes lengths $\sqrt{\lambda_j^l}$, and a residual variance σ_j^2 (in any direction orthogonal to the span of the principal axes). The $\mathbf{w}_j^l$ are the eigenvectors of a local principal component analysis, and the λ_j^l are the corresponding eigenvalues. The hyper-ellipsoids are iso-potential surfaces of the normalized Mahalanobis distance plus reconstruction error (see section 3.2.1),

$$E_j(\mathbf{z}) = \mathbf{y}_j^T \Lambda_j^{-1} \mathbf{y}_j + \frac{1}{\sigma_j^2}(\boldsymbol{\xi}_j^T \boldsymbol{\xi}_j - \mathbf{y}_j^T \mathbf{y}_j) + \ln \det \Lambda_j + (d-q) \ln \sigma_j^2 \ . \quad (4.1)$$

The dimensionality of the pattern space is d, and q is the number of principal components. $\boldsymbol{\xi}_j$ is the displacement from the center, $\boldsymbol{\xi}_j = \mathbf{z} - \mathbf{c}_j$. Its representation in the local coordinate system of the ellipsoid is $\mathbf{y}_j = \mathbf{W}_j^T \boldsymbol{\xi}_j$. The eigenvectors $\mathbf{w}_j^l$ are the columns of $\mathbf{W}_j$. Λ_j is a diagonal matrix containing the eigenvalues λ_j^l.

An input to the network (one part of the components of $\mathbf{p}$) defines the offset of a constrained space $\mathbf{z}(\boldsymbol{\eta})$ spanning the space of all possible output values:

$$\mathbf{z}(\boldsymbol{\eta}) = \mathbf{M}\boldsymbol{\eta} + \mathbf{p} \ . \tag{4.2}$$

$\boldsymbol{\eta}$ is a collection of s free parameters (s being the dimension of the network output). $\mathbf{M}$ is a $d \times s$ matrix, which is chosen such that the constrained space is aligned with the coordinate axes.

The recall of the complete pattern happens in two steps. First, for each unit j, determine the point $\hat{\mathbf{z}}_j$ that yields the smallest potential value (4.1) on the constrained subspace. Second, choose the unit j^* that gives the smallest of these minimal potential values $\{E_j(\hat{\mathbf{z}}_j)\}$. The corresponding $\hat{\mathbf{z}}_{j^*}$ yields the desired output values (figure 4.2).

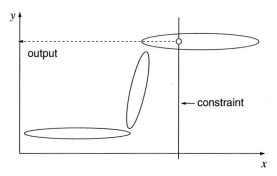

Figure 4.2:   Pattern recall. The ellipses are iso-potential curves of the error measure E_j for each unit j. The input x defines the constraint's offset from zero. In this subspace, the unit j^* and the point (circle) that result in the smallest error E_{j^*} are chosen. This point's y value is the desired output.

The error E_j as a function of the free parameters $\boldsymbol{\eta}$ can be written as:

$$
\begin{aligned}
E_j(\mathbf{z}(\boldsymbol{\eta})) \ = \ & (\mathbf{M}\boldsymbol{\eta} + \boldsymbol{\pi}_j)^T (\mathbf{W}_j \boldsymbol{\Lambda}_j^{-1} \mathbf{W}_j^T + \frac{1}{\sigma_j^2} \{ \mathbf{I} - \mathbf{W}_j \mathbf{W}_j^T \}) \, (\mathbf{M}\boldsymbol{\eta} + \boldsymbol{\pi}_j) \\
& + \ \ln \det \boldsymbol{\Lambda}_j + (d - q) \ln \sigma_j^2 \ ,
\end{aligned} \tag{4.3}
$$

with $\boldsymbol{\pi}_j = \mathbf{p} - \mathbf{c}_j$. We derive with respect to $\boldsymbol{\eta}$:

$$\frac{\partial E_j}{\partial \boldsymbol{\eta}} = 2 \, \mathbf{M}^T \mathbf{D}_j \mathbf{M} \boldsymbol{\eta} + 2 \, \mathbf{M}^T \mathbf{D}_j \boldsymbol{\pi}_j \tag{4.4}$$

with

$$\mathbf{D}_j = \mathbf{W}_j \boldsymbol{\Lambda}_j^{-1} \mathbf{W}_j^T + \frac{1}{\sigma_j^2} \left(\mathbf{I} - \mathbf{W}_j \mathbf{W}_j^T \right) \ . \tag{4.5}$$

Setting the derivative equal to zero yields,

$$\hat{\boldsymbol{\eta}}_j = \mathbf{A}_j(\mathbf{p} - \mathbf{c}_j) \tag{4.6}$$

with

$$\mathbf{A}_j = -(\mathbf{M}^T\mathbf{D}_j\mathbf{M})^{-1}\mathbf{M}^T\mathbf{D}_j \ . \tag{4.7}$$

After the input and output dimensions have been selected, $\mathbf{A}_j$ needs to be computed only once for each unit.

The function $E(\boldsymbol{\eta})$ is convex. Therefore, $\hat{\boldsymbol{\eta}}_j$ is the only minimum. Thus, $\hat{\mathbf{z}}_j = \mathbf{M}\hat{\boldsymbol{\eta}}_j + \mathbf{p}$ is the point with the smallest potential on the constraint. Next, j^* can be chosen, and the resulting $\hat{\mathbf{z}}_{j^*}$ concludes the algorithm. For each input a unique output is given, and local minima as described in section 4.1.2 are avoided.

4.3 Function approximation on synthetic data

To demonstrate the working of the recall algorithm, it was tested on two synthetic pattern distributions, a noisy sine wave and a noisy circle. For both distributions, the mixture of local PCA was gained by using the algorithm MPPCA-ext (section 3.3). However, the alternative algorithm NGPCA (section 3.2) could have been also used; the results were similar.

The sine-wave distribution is composed of 800 points. The mixture model contained nine ellipses with two principal components each. Figure 4.3 shows the result of the recall if the x-coordinate was given. The recall is locally linear and discontinuities occur between the changes from one ellipse to the next. On a global scale, the sine-wave is correctly restored.

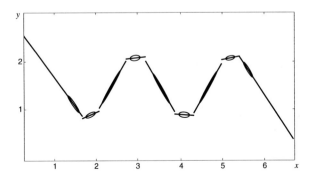

Figure 4.3: Input-output relations (thick lines). The input is on the x-axis. The nine ellipses were trained on a sine-wave (data not shown).

The second test illustrates the two advantages over feed-forward networks, like multi-layer perceptrons. The distribution consists of 1000 points arranged in a noisy circle with radius 1.0 (figure 4.4). It was approximated by six ellipses with two eigenvectors each. Figure 4.4 shows the results of the recall for two different directions ($x \rightarrow y$ and $y \rightarrow x$) using the same mixture of local PCA. The mapping in both directions is redundant (one-to-many). Nevertheless, the algorithm finds a valid solution that lies on the distribution of training patterns for input values in the training domain. Here, the solution jumps between the two semicircles. In contrast, a multi-layer perceptron would average over redundant solutions, and thus, it would learn to produce a line going through the middle of the circle.

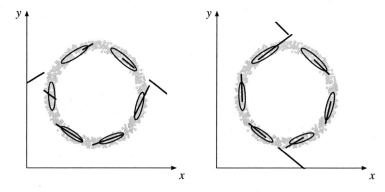

Figure 4.4: Input-output relations (thick lines). In the left figure, the input is on the x-axis, and in the right figure, the input is on the y-axis.

4.4   Image Completion

The abstract RNN can be used to complete partially occluded images. The completion was first tested on small windows cut out from natural backgrounds, and second tested on human faces. To use the recall mechanism, the gray-scaled images need to be converted into data points (vectors). This conversion was achieved by writing an image row by row into a vector (pixel values scaled between 0 and 1).

4.4.1   Windows from natural scenes

The recall algorithm was applied to blind spot interpolation. A square cut out from an image window was filled given the surrounding pixels.

Methods

The images were taken from the background data set[1] from the 'Computational Vision' group at Caltech, Pasadena. The set comprises 396 images of size 223×147 pixels showing indoor and outdoor scenes. To create the training set, 200 windows 10×10 pixels large were cut out at random positions from each of these images. Thus, totally, 79 200 100-dimensional training patterns were created. The background data set also comprises images of size 378×251. Three of them were used for testing.

The local PCA methods used for training, NGPCA, NGPCA-constV, and MPPCA-ext contained ten units and extracted 50 principal components. The NGPCA parameters were $\rho(0) = 10.0$, $\rho(t_{max}) = 0.0001$, $\epsilon(0) = 0.5$, $\epsilon(t_{max}) = 0.001$, and $t_{max} = 400\,000$. The mixture models were compared, first, to a model using a single unit extracting either 50 or all 100 eigenvectors, but with the same recall algorithm, and, second, to a multi-layer perceptron (MLP). The MLP had 64 input, 30 hidden, and 36 output neurons. The corresponding activation functions were the identity, the sigmoid function, and again the identity. The weights were initialized with random values drawn uniformly from the interval $[-0.1; 0.1]$. 2 000 steps of resilient propagation (Riedmiller and Braun, 1993) were used for training.

Unless otherwise noted, a center square of size 6×6 pixels defines the output, and the pixels surrounding this square are the input. To illustrate the performance of the recall, 850 such squares were cut out of two test images (figure 4.7), and the abstract RNN completed all of them individually. It was ensured that a two pixels wide border (used as input) remained around each hole. The restored test images were compared to images gained by filling each hole with a color that is the average over all border-pixel gray-values. For quantitative performance tests, 5 000 windows were cut out at random positions from another test image. The mean square error between a recalled window and the corresponding original window was calculated as the average over all output pixels and test windows.

Results

All training methods of the abstract RNN had similar errors and showed about the same performance than an MLP (table 4.1). NGPCA was slightly better than NGPCA-constV and the single unit (all other comparisons did not show a significant difference).

The remaining results were gained by using NGPCA for training. On individual image windows, the abstract RNN could complete structures like edges and uniform surfaces, but isolated structures in the center square could

---

[1]The data are from http://www.vision.caltech.edu/html-files/archive.html.

training method	SE
NGPCA	0.0036
NGPCA-constV	0.0039
MPPCA-ext	0.0037
single unit ($q = 100$)	0.0039
single unit ($q = 50$)	0.0042
MLP	0.0037

Table 4.1: Average square error per pixel (SE) for each training method. The standard error for all mean values was around 0.0001.

not be foreseen (figure 4.5). The two test images with 850 holes could be completed to almost the quality of the original images (figure 4.7). However, tilted edges and the details of leaves could not be completed correctly.

The MLP can learn only one recall direction (at once). However, for the abstract RNN, arbitrary pixels can be chosen as input (figure 4.6).

Figure 4.5: Four randomly chosen recall examples. In each pair of images, the left one shows the original image, and the right one presents the recall result. The square encloses the pixels marked as output.

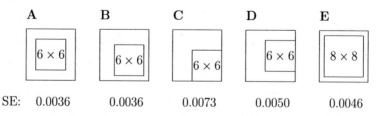

Figure 4.6: Mean square error per pixel (SE) for different output windows. For A, B, D, and E the standard error was about 0.0001, and 0.0002 for C.

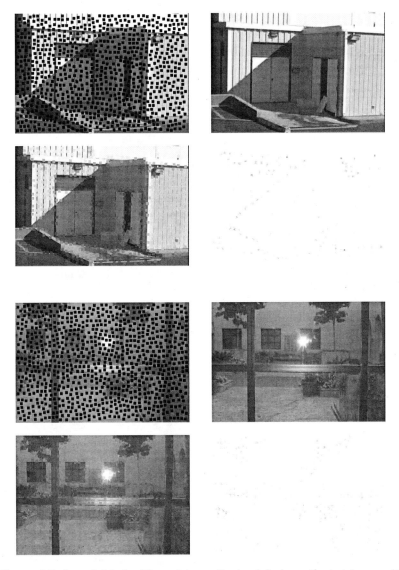

Figure 4.7: In each block of four pictures, the top left shows the test image with 850 holes, the top right shows the restored image using the abstract RNN, the bottom left shows the restored image using the average color (see text), and the bottom right shows the absolute difference between the RNN restored image and the original test image (white = 0, black = 1).

4.4.2   Faces

Image completion with the abstract RNN was tested on the completion of partially occluded faces. Here, a pattern consists of the image of a whole face.

Methods

The faces were taken from the faces database[2] of the Max Planck Institute for Biological Cybernetics, Tübingen (Blanz and Vetter, 1999). The database contains 100 male and 100 female faces, each in seven different perspectives (thus, in total 1400 images). The images are in color and their size is 256×256 pixels. The faces are centered in each image and the background is black. 90% of the male and female faces were used for training and the remainder for testing (1260 training patterns and 140 test patterns).

To preprocess each image, first, a gray-scaled image was obtained by averaging over all color channels. Second, a margin 45 pixels wide (mostly black) was removed. Then, the image was subsampled to a 26×26 image. In the subsampled image, each pixel corresponds to a window (6×6 pixels) in the image of the previous processing stage. The pixel's gray-value was set to the average gray-value in that window.

In training, the mixture models NGPCA and NGPCA-constV contained ten units with ten principal components each. The models had the same training parameters as in section 4.4.1. MPPCA-ext could not be used because the dimensionality of the patterns was too high (see section 3.5). Results were again compared to a model using a single unit. 119 principal components were extracted, resulting in the same number of free parameters as for the mixture model. Moreover, the results were compared to a table look-up, herein from the training set, the image was chosen that had the smallest Euclidean distance to an input pattern.

Results

The mixture models showed about the same performance (table 4.2). They did better than the single unit on large concatenated output regions; the single unit was better to interpolate between thin stripes. All variants of the abstract RNN were better than a table look-up on the training set.

The completions obtained by the abstract RNN resembled human faces (figure 4.8, here, NGPCA was used as example). Some of the recalled images that do not match their test image (like the images in the bottom row) nevertheless seem to fit the boundary conditions. These cases suggest that

---

[2]The database is available at http://faces.kyb.tuebingen.mpg.de.

training method	▀ SE	▨ SE	▬ SE
NGPCA	0.0133	0.0056	0.0093
NGPCA-constV	0.0129	0.0056	0.0090
single unit	0.0144	0.0042	0.0110
table look-up	0.0202	0.0118	0.0158

Table 4.2: Average square error per pixel (SE) for each training method and for three different masks (black pixels mark output dimensions). The standard error for all mean values was around 5%.

the approximation of the distribution of faces intersects the constraint space more than once. To exploit this one-to-many mapping, the ellipsoid (unit) was determined that yields the second smallest potential (see section 4.2) and the square error of the corresponding completion was computed. Using NGPCA, for the first mask (top half occluded), in 18 cases, the second ellipsoid provided the solution that matched better the test image (smaller square error). Replacing the corresponding originally recalled images by these cases, the mean square error dropped from 0.0133 to 0.0122.

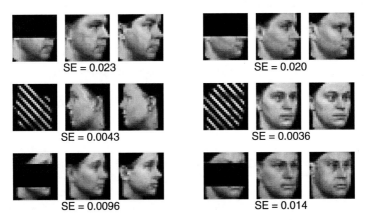

SE = 0.023   SE = 0.020

SE = 0.0043   SE = 0.0036

SE = 0.0096   SE = 0.014

Figure 4.8: Recall on randomly chosen faces. Each group of three images shows the input on the left, the output in the middle, and the complete test image for comparison on the right. The square error per pixel (SE) between recalled image and test image is given.

4.5   Kinematic arm model

The abstract RNN can be used to learn the kinematics of a robot arm (Hoffmann and Möller, 2003). Here, a pattern consists of the coordinates of the end-effector, the joint angles of the arm, and a binary collision variable. By completion of a pattern that only includes the end-effector coordinates and the collision state, a set of joint angles can be obtained; this is the inverse direction. Analogously, the forward direction maps from the joint angles to the end-effector coordinates and the collision state. For a given end-effector position, redundant arm postures exist. Apart from performance tests for the inverse and forward directions, two further tests show that the abstract RNN can cope with additional noise dimensions (see also section 3.1) and that the performance of the abstract RNN depends on the number of input dimensions.

4.5.1   Methods

A robot arm with six rotatory degrees of freedom was simulated. It corresponds to the real robot arm in chapter 6. Figure 4.9 shows the setup of the model. By modeling the geometry of the arm and its surrounding, it could be determined if a collision occurred between different parts of the arm or between the arm and the surrounding obstacles. This information was used for the binary collision variable.

The training set was generated by randomly choosing 50 000 joint-angle sets (each set contains six angles). Angles were chosen from a uniform interval of ± 120 degrees centered at a predefined zero position. For each joint-angle set, the end-effector position was determined from the geometric arm model. It was also calculated if the angle set resulted in a collision. Thus, each training pattern is 10-dimensional and contains six joint angles, three end-effector coordinates, and one collision variable. Only training patterns with an end-effector position inside a workspace of $500 \times 500 \times 500\,\text{mm}$ above the table were included in the training set. Moreover, the patterns were chosen such that half of the set were collision trials and half no-collision trials. All values were scaled to fit in a 10-dimensional cube with side length one.

The training parameters for NGPCA and NGPCA-const were the same as in section 4.4.1. In most tests (apart from those that did show the dependence on m or q), the local PCA mixture models contained $m = 200$ units and $q = 6$ principal components. Neural Gas (Martinetz et al., 1993) was used as an alternative training method (the same training parameters as for NGPCA were used). It was composed of 980 code-book vectors, resulting in the same number of free parameters as used for the mixture model. By setting the potential of the code-book vectors to the Euclidean distance, the same recall

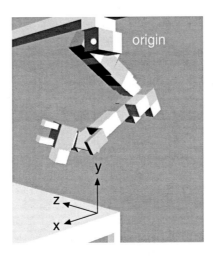

Figure 4.9: Simulated robot arm. Location of the origin and axes of the end-effector coordinate system are shown.

algorithm could be used as for the local PCA method. The abstract RNN was further compared to a multi-layer perceptron that had one hidden layer with 200 neurons (smaller or higher numbers did not improve the performance). In the hidden layer, a sigmoid activation function was used. The weights were initialized with random values drawn uniformly from the interval $[-0.5; 0.5]$. Forward and inverse direction had to be learned separately. In both cases, the network trained 2 000 epochs of resilient propagation (Riedmiller and Braun, 1993).

The local dimensionality of the kinematic manifold is six (the six joint angles are the free parameters), and this guided the choice of the parameter q. In general, however, the local dimensionality of a data distribution is not known a priori. To obtain the number of dimensions, the following algorithm was used.

For every data point, the 30 closest (Euclidean distance) neighbors were selected. Then, on each neighborhood a PCA was carried out. The resulting eigenvalues were averaged over all data points. The size of successive averaged eigenvalues λ_q is expected to decrease slowly until the local dimensionality is reached, and then, this size breaks down and reaches a noise level. Thus, the local dimensionality can be obtained as the position of the first peak in the series λ_{q+1}/λ_q (Philipona et al., 2003).

The trained abstract RNN could recall in both inverse and forward directions. For the inverse direction, the end-effector coordinates and the collision state are the offset of a constrained space, and the recall algorithm had to find the joint angles. Position errors were calculated between the desired end-effector coordinates and the ones obtained by feeding the recalled joint angles into the geometric arm model. Collision errors were obtained in a similar way. Desired end-effector coordinates were taken from a $11 \times 11 \times 11$ grid inside the working space.

In the forward direction, the six joint angles were given, and the network had to find the end-effector coordinates and the collision state. The position error and collision-prediction error were computed by directly comparing the network output with the result from the geometrical model. The test pattern set used here was randomly generated in the same way as the training set. It contained 1331 patterns (the same number as for the inverse direction).

Two further tests show how the abstract RNN copes with additional noise dimensions and how the recall results depend on the dimensionality of the input. For the first of these tests, another training set was generated with three additional noise dimensions. In this set, each training pattern had three additional variables, whose values were randomly drawn from the interval $[-1.0; 1.0]$.

To investigate the effect of the number of input dimensions on the performance, errors were computed for arbitrary recall directions. In a test with arbitrary directions that include one-to-many mappings, as in the case of the inverse direction, a recalled pattern cannot be directly compared with a test pattern. Moreover, no function exists that could map the output back onto the input (to compute the error as above). As a solution, the square error was computed as the minimal squared distance to the manifold given by the geometric arm model. This optimization (in the subspace of joint-angles) was carried out with the 'Downhill Simplex Method' (Press et al., 1993, p. 408). The square error was computed on all test patterns for each possible number of input dimensions, while for each test pattern, the single input dimensions were chosen at random. This random choice avoids geometric effects that might favor specific directions.

4.5.2 Results

The abstract RNN could cope with the redundant arm postures for a given end-effector position; the MLP could not (table 4.3). The local PCA mixture approximated the training data also better then Neural Gas (table 4.3). The results from the different mixture models NGPCA, NGPCA-constV, and MPPCA-ext were almost equal (table 4.3). Compared to NGPCA, NGPCA-constV was slightly worse on the inverse direction. Over five different training cycles (retraining of the mixture of local PCA), the average position errors varied only slightly (for NGPCA, the maximum deviation was 2 mm).

method	direction	input	position error (mm)	collision error (%)
NGPCA	inverse	no collision	27 ± 15	5
NGPCA	inverse	collision	23 ± 13	8
NGPCA	forward	-	44 ± 27	11
NGPCA-constV	inverse	no collision	31 ± 17	5
NGPCA-constV	inverse	collision	28 ± 14	11
NGPCA-constV	forward	-	43 ± 29	11
MPPCA-ext	inverse	no collision	29 ± 15	5
MPPCA-ext	inverse	collision	25 ± 14	6
MPPCA-ext	forward	-	45 ± 29	14
Neural Gas	inverse	no collision	58 ± 26	2
Neural Gas	inverse	collision	56 ± 27	4
Neural Gas	forward	-	160 ± 74	18
MLP	inverse	no collision	310 ± 111	30
MLP	forward	-	93 ± 48	13

Table 4.3: Position and collision errors for an abstract RNN using NGPCA, NGPCA-constV, and MPPCA-ext for training, compared to a variant using Neural Gas for training and to a multilayer perceptron (MLP). Results are shown for two different directions of recall: forward and inverse. The inverse model takes the desired collision state as an additional input variable (third column). Position errors are averaged over all test patterns, and are given with standard deviations. In the inverse case, the collision error is the percentage of trials deviating from the collision input value. In the forward case, it is the erroneous number of collision state predictions.

The mixture models distribute the training patterns among the units of the mixture. For NGPCA and NGPCA-constV, every pattern is assigned to one unit (at the end of the training). The number of patterns assigned to a unit is a measure for the weight of the unit; for MPPCA-ext, the weights are the prior probabilities. These weights had roughly a bell-shaped distribution among the units (figure 4.10). Different from MPPCA-ext, the distributions for NGPCA and NGPCA-constV showed a second peak for units having few assigned patterns (around 50, the average is 250). A single peak seems to be favorable. However, the distribution of assigned patterns also depends on the structure of the data set (which is largely unknown). Apparently, in this experiment, the effect on the performance was negligible (table 4.3).

The remaining tests were carried out only with NGPCA. The distribution of the individual errors shows regions corresponding to different ellipsoids selected during the recall (figure 4.11). At the transition between two regions, the error as a function of the input is discontinuous.

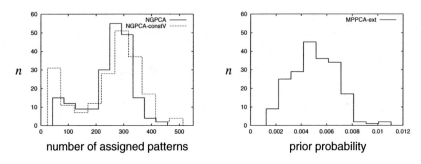

Figure 4.10: Histogram of assigned patterns, respective prior probabilities. n is the number of units for each interval.

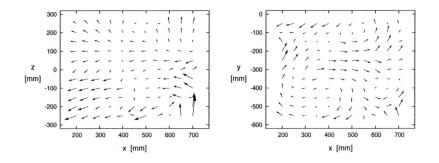

Figure 4.11: Position errors of the inverse model with input 'collision'. (Left) Horizontal plane (approximately 70 mm above the table). (Right) Vertical plane through the origin $(z = 0)$.

   The performance depends on the number of units m and principal components q. The position and the collision errors decreased with increasing m (table 4.4). Furthermore, the position error was smallest at $q = 6$ (figure 4.12, right). This q value matches the local dimensionality of the distribution (figure 4.12, left).

   The abstract RNN could also cope with additional noise dimensions if the number of principal components was adjusted accordingly (table 4.5). With three noise dimensions and $q = 6$ principal components, the position errors of the abstract RNN were more than double . However, with $q = 9$, the position errors were again at the no-noise level.

direction	input	error	$m = 50$	$m = 100$	$m = 200$
inverse	no collision	position (mm)	48	38	27
inverse	no collision	collision (%)	5	5	5
inverse	collision	position (mm)	47	35	23
inverse	collision	collision (%)	8	9	8
forward	-	position (mm)	74	56	44
forward	-	collision (%)	16	14	11

Table 4.4: Dependence on the number m of units.

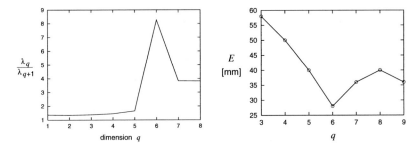

Figure 4.12: (Left) Ratio of successive averaged eigenvalues λ_q and λ_{q+1} (see methods). (Right) Dependence of the position error E (here for the direction: inverse, no collision) on the number of principal components q.

direction	input	error	$q = 6$ (no noise)	$q = 6$	$q = 9$
inverse	no collision	position (mm)	27	57	30
inverse	no collision	collision (%)	5	6	6
inverse	collision	position (mm)	23	64	24
inverse	collision	collision (%)	8	6	11
forward	-	position (mm)	44	101	45
forward	-	collision (%)	11	15	13

Table 4.5: Compensation of noise. The first column of numbers shows the result without noise dimensions (as in table 4.3), the second with three noise dimensions and six principal components, and the third with noise and nine principal components.

The errors for the forward direction were consistently higher than for the inverse direction (table 4.3 and 4.4). The major difference seems to be that the forward direction has six input dimensions; the inverse direction has only four. This is consistent with the finding that the square error per output dimension increased with the number of input dimensions (figure 4.13). For intermediate numbers r, the increase was even exponential. In the following section, this finding is investigated theoretically.

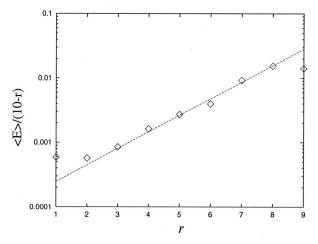

Figure 4.13: Mean square error (SE) as a function of the number r of input dimensions. The dashed line is the function $a \exp(br)$ fitted to point 2 to 8; b was 0.59 ± 0.03.

4.6   Dependence on the number of input dimensions

As shown in section 4.5, the performance of the abstract recurrent neural network depends on the number of input dimensions chosen. A higher number of input dimensions results in a higher sum of square errors per pattern. This relationship is investigated theoretically on a simplified abstract RNN.

The first simplification is that the model consists of spheres instead of ellipsoids. Thus, the distribution of training data is approximated by a set of m code-book vectors $\mathbf{c}^j$, and for each of them the potential field is given by the Euclidean distance. The second simplification is that the code-book vectors are uniformly randomly distributed. This is justified for distributions that are wrapped inside the pattern space, and are not restricted to embedded hyper-planes, as it is likely the case for the kinematic arm model. Recall works as in section 4.2 (see also figure 4.14).

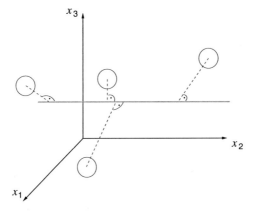

Figure 4.14: The trained abstract network consists of a set of code-book vectors, here illustrated as circles. These vectors are distributed randomly. Recall happens by finding the closest vector to a constraint space (gray line). The offset of this line from the origin is the input.

We assume that the code-book vectors lie inside a d-dimensional cube of side length two, centered at the origin. Since the code-book vectors are distributed uniformly, the average error is independent of the specific value of the input (offset of the constrained space)[3]. Thus, we arrange the constrained spaces such that they all go through the origin. If $d - 1$ input dimensions are given, the constraint is the x_d-axis. For $d - 2$ input dimensions the axis x_d and x_{d-1} span the constraint space, and so on (see figure 4.15 as an example). Instead of choosing different input values to compute the sum of square errors, we draw a new set of $\mathbf{c}^j$ from a random distribution for each test trial.

Given r input dimensions, the squared distance E^j of $\mathbf{c}^j$ to the constrained space is

$$E^j = \sum_{i=1}^{r} \left(c_i^j\right)^2 . \tag{4.8}$$

We define the square error E as the minimum squared distance to the data approximation (in the kinematic arm model, this matches the computation of the square error in the case of arbitrary directions, see section 4.5.1). Thus,

---

[3]Boundary effects are ignored. For large m, they probably have only a minor effect.

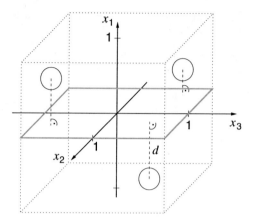

Figure 4.15: Example using $r = 1$ input dimensions in a $n = 3$ dimensional space. The x_2x_3 plane is the constrained space. Code-book vectors are illustrated as circles. Possible code-book locations are enclosed by the cube drawn with dotted lines. The dashed lines show the distances between constraint and code-book vectors.

$$E = \min\left\{\sum_{i=1}^{r}(c_i^1)^2, \sum_{i=1}^{r}(c_i^2)^2, \ldots, \sum_{i=1}^{r}(c_i^m)^2\right\} \ . \tag{4.9}$$

The sum of square errors per pattern is the expectation value of E given a random distribution of $\mathbf{c}^j$. To compute the expectation of a minimum, we use the following trick (Wentzell, 2003). The cumulative probability $P_c(T)$ that all E^j are larger than a threshold T is computed. $P_c(T)$ is monotone descending, starting with $P_c(0) = 1$. The negative derivative of $P_c(T)$ can be interpreted as the probability density function of T. For a given T, this function provides the probability density that T equals the smallest member of the set $\{E^j\}$. Thus, the expectation value of T (the first momentum of the probability density function) equals the expectation value of E, the minimum of $\{E^j\}$. Therefore,

$$\langle E \rangle = \langle T \rangle = -\int \frac{dP_c(T)}{dT} T \, dT \ . \tag{4.10}$$

The probability p that a point $\mathbf{c}^j$ has a squared distance E^j larger or equal to T is the cube volume outside the r-sphere[4] with radius $\sqrt{T}$ centered at the

---

[4]An r-sphere is a hyper-sphere embedded in an r-dimensional space.

origin divided by the cube volume (figure 4.16). The cumulative probability P_c is p to the power of m.

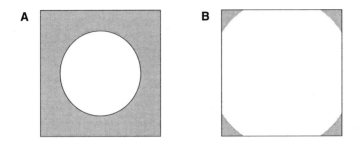

Figure 4.16: The gray area relative to the total area of the square is the probability that a point lies outside the circle. Two examples with different radii are shown.

To make the function p over T analytically integrable, we make an approximation. The r-cube, the space of all possible codebook vectors (in the first r dimensions), is replaced by an r-sphere with radius $\sqrt{r}$ centered at the origin. This sphere encloses tightly the r-cube. To compensate this step, we multiply the number of codebook vectors m with the r-sphere volume divided by the r-cube volume. The volume of an r-sphere with unit radius can be written as

$$V_r = \frac{\pi^{\frac{r}{2}}}{\Gamma(\frac{r}{2} + 1)} \; . \tag{4.11}$$

Γ is the Gamma-function. It is related to the factorial by $\Gamma(n) = (n-1)!$ for positive integers n. For $r = 2$, for example, the above volume V_r equals π. Hence, the resulting volume relation v^r (here, for the sphere radius $\sqrt{r}$) is

$$v^r = \frac{\pi^{\frac{r}{2}} r^{\frac{r}{2}}}{\Gamma(\frac{r}{2} + 1) 2^r} \; . \tag{4.12}$$

The above step is justified by the uniform distribution of the $\mathbf{c}^j$. But, it is not an equivalence transformation (for $r > 1$). The quality of this approximation will be tested later. The resulting number of vectors, $\mu = \mathrm{int}(v^r m)$, is rounded to an integer value. With the approximation, the probability $p(T)$ that a vector has a squared distance $E^j \geq T$ can be expressed as

$$p(T) = 1 - \frac{\sqrt{T}^r}{\sqrt{r}^r} \; . \tag{4.13}$$

The total probability P_c that all vectors fulfill the above condition is

$$P_c(T) = \prod_{j=1}^{\mu} p(T) = (1 - (\frac{T}{r})^{\frac{r}{2}})^{\mu} \; . \tag{4.14}$$

The value of T extends from 0 to r. Using (4.10), we obtain for the expectation value of E

$$\langle E \rangle = -\int_0^r \frac{dP_c(T)}{dT} T \, dT = \int_0^r P_c(T) dT - P_c(T)T \Big|_0^r = \int_0^r P_c(T) dT \; . \tag{4.15}$$

The second equality sign uses integration by parts, the last equality sign uses (4.14). The final integration, using (4.14), gives

$$\langle E \rangle = r \frac{\Gamma(\frac{r+2}{r})\Gamma(\mu+1)}{\Gamma(\frac{2+r+\mu r}{r})} \; . \tag{4.16}$$

The integral was solved with the help of MATLAB® and its symbolic toolbox. Using the equality $\Gamma(x) = (x-1)\Gamma(x-1)$, the expression can be simplified to

$$\langle E \rangle = r \prod_{j=1}^{\mu} \frac{j}{j+2/r} \; . \tag{4.17}$$

For large μ, the latter is more feasible for numerical evaluation than (4.16). We further investigate the quality of our approximation. The case $m = 1$ can be evaluated correctly. For one codebook vector, the expectation of its squared distance can be directly calculated:

$$\langle E \rangle = 2^{-r} \int_{-1}^{1} \int_{-1}^{1} \cdots \int_{-1}^{1} \sum_{i=1}^{r} c_i^2 \prod_{i=1}^{r} dc_i = 2^{-r} r \frac{2^r}{3} = \frac{r}{3} \; . \tag{4.18}$$

Figure 4.17 shows the result of this comparison. The mismatch increases with the number of input dimensions r.

We want to check our approximation using larger m. The result from (4.12) and (4.17) was compared to a simulation, in which $\mathbf{c}^j$ were drawn randomly from a r-cube with side length 2. Figure 4.18 shows the result, using $r = 10$ input dimensions and 100 000 trials for each m value in the simulation. The approximation got better the more codebook vectors were used. The number of codebook vectors needed for a good approximation depends on the value of r. The higher r, the more vectors are needed.

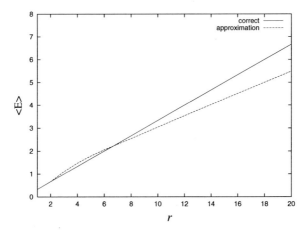

Figure 4.17: Comparison between the approximation, replacing the r-cube by a r-sphere resulting in (4.12) and (4.17), and the correctly evaluated result (4.18) for one code-book vector.

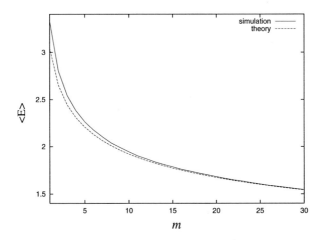

Figure 4.18: Comparison between the theory, using (4.12) and (4.17), and the result from a simulation, with $r = 10$. The number of code-book vectors is m.

Finally, the dependency on the number of input dimensions is demonstrated for the case $m = 200$. As above, the theory is compared to a simulation, using $100\,000$ trials for each r value. In this test, theory and simulation results did overlap (figure 4.19). Between $r = 5$ and $r = 8$ the increase is approximately exponential with exponent 0.69.

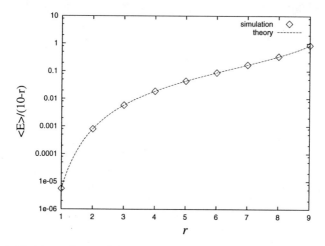

Figure 4.19: Dependency of the mean square error per output dimension on the number of input dimensions r for $m = 200$ ($d = 10$). Theory, using (4.12) and (4.17), and simulation results are shown.

4.7   Discussion

A pattern association model, called abstract recurrent neural network, was introduced that works analogue to an RNN. Like feed-forward networks, the model can be trained on any data distribution. It has, however, two advantages over feed-forward networks. First, a trained abstract RNN can associate patterns in any mapping direction. Second, the model can cope with one-to-many mappings.

The recall algorithm works on top of a mixture of local PCA (geometrically a mixture of ellipsoids) that approximates the data distribution. Different from a gradient descent relaxation, the algorithm avoids local minimum since an analytical solution exists that maps an input pattern directly onto its completion. The algorithm is further independent of the method that produced the mixture model, and in all examples from this chapter, also the recall results were similar for different local PCA methods.

The mapping obtained by the abstract RNN is locally linear. At the transition between two ellipsoids the mapping is discontinuous (figure 4.3 and 4.11). Avoiding these discontinuities might improve the algorithm. One possibility may be to interpolate between neighboring ellipsoids. Here, however, the difficulty is to find a neighbor that can continue the solution instead of providing an alternative solution (interpolating between alternative solutions leads to errors). Figure 4.20 shows a possible problem. The neighbor ellipse with the alternative solution can have the smallest Euclidean and Mahalanobis distance to the current ellipse.

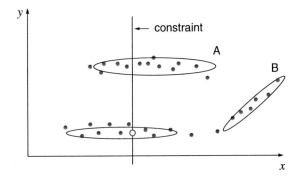

Figure 4.20: An interpolation algorithm needs to find a neighboring ellipse for the current relaxation result (circle). In this example, however, ellipse A (representing an alternative solution) is closer to the current ellipse than ellipse B, which would be favorable.

Tavan et al. (1990) suggested another recall algorithm based on a density model of the training patterns. Here, the density is a mixture of uniform Gaussian functions. Recall happens in a recurrent radial basis function network. Its activation functions are the Gaussians from the local densities. Thus, the current state is a weighted sum of the Gaussian centers. To avoid local minima, the algorithm anneals (shrinks) the width of the Gaussians parallel to the recurrent state update. For the constrained recall, however, a straight-forward extension of this algorithm to ellipsoids did not have a comparable performance as the abstract RNN (figure 4.21). The extension consists of three parts: the uniform Gaussians are replaced by multi-variate ones (2.16); the updated state is projected onto the constrained space, and the annealing is realized by coupling all eigenvalues to a global σ value ($\lambda' = \lambda + \mu(\sigma - \lambda)$ with the coupling μ; σ is kept constant, while μ

slowly decreases during the annealing). The completion did not follow the shape of the tilted ellipses because the weighted sum of centers came out to be the center of only one ellipse; if a state is close enough to one ellipse, the activation of the other ellipses can be neglected.

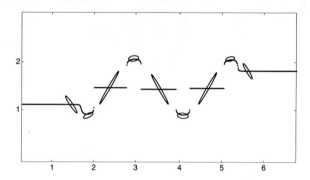

Figure 4.21: Pattern completion based on the recurrent radial basis function network suggested by Tavan et al. (1990). The recall cannot follow the shape of the ellipses (compare with figure 4.3). The thick curves and dots show the input-output relation. The input is on the x-axis.

The abstract RNN could be successfully applied to the completion of images (section 4.4). In comparison, a discrete or continuous Hopfield network (Hopfield, 1982, 1984) cannot be used to recall gray-scaled images. On the face completion task, the abstract RNN was even better then a table look-up on the whole training set.

On the completion of small windows, the mixture of local PCA resulted in about the same recall error as a single unit. With both single and mixture model, the recalled images seem to capture only the low-pass filtered image part. They are averages over all windows that match the input pixels. Moreover, the midpoints of the mixture model came out to be just monotone gray tones. Apparently, the distribution of images just extends from the origin into different subspaces. Thus, the advantage of having different unit centers is lost.

On the faces, the mixture model was better than a single unit if large connected areas needed to be filled. Here, multiple solutions can exists for a given input, and the mixture model could cover the different solutions. However, if only thin stripes needed to be filled, the solution is not ambiguous, and here, the single unit was better.

The abstract RNN could learn the kinematics of a robot arm (section 4.5). The inverse direction had redundant degrees of freedom. Nevertheless, the model could recall a posture that brought the end-effector to a given position; a multi-layer perceptron could not. All mixture of local PCA variants did almost equally well. In this experiment, NGPCA did not produce dead units (units with no patterns assigned to); the smallest number of patterns for one unit was around 50 (figure 4.10). This possibly explains why NGPCA-constV did not bring an improvement (see section 3.2.2). The slight decrease in performance for NGPCA-constV might result from ellipsoids that erroneously connect distant parts of the distribution, as observed in figure 3.8.C. These ellipsoids have only a few assigned patterns, and this might explain, why NGPCA-constV results in a lower minimal number of assigned patterns per unit (figure 4.10).

The following rules can be given for the number of units m and principal components q. Increasing m increased the performance because the training patterns lie on a manifold that is non-linear. A stable training, however, limits the maximum number of units (this depends on the number of training patterns). The optimal number of principal components was equal to the local dimensionality of the distribution. For arbitrary distributions, the local dimensionality can be obtained by computing a PCA on a local neighborhood within the distribution (section 4.5.1 and figure 4.12, left).

For an optimal performance, it was expected that the local dimensionality sets the minimum value for q because fewer principal components cannot describe the local extend of the distribution. However, it was not expected that further increasing q decreased the performance. An explanation might be that the eigenvalues in the direction orthogonal to the kinematic manifold were unequal (figure 4.12, left). Thus, for $q > 6$ the error measure (4.1) is not isotropic for directions orthogonal to the manifold (as it should be ideally), and this may disturb the competition between the units in the recall algorithm.

The abstract RNN could cope with additional noise dimensions. If they are added, the pattern distribution also extends to these dimensions. Thus, the local dimensionality increases by the number of added noise dimensions, and q needs to be adjusted accordingly to get the same performance.

The mean error of the recall increased with the number r of input dimensions given a constant m. This increase was observed in the experiment with the kinematic arm model and in a simplified stochastic version of the abstract RNN. Both tests could produce an exponential increase for intermediate values of r (figure 4.13 and 4.19). Moreover, the exponent was of the same order (0.59 in experiment compared to 0.69 in theory), despite the rough simplifications made in the theory. Thus, the increase in error with increasing r is possibly a characteristic of the recall algorithm. Therefore, in applications, mappings from many dimensions to only a few (for example, ten to two) should be avoided.

In chapter 6 the abstract RNN is applied to a real robot arm. There, the robot's task is to grasp an object, and the RNN associates an arm posture with an image of the object.

Chapter 5

Kernel PCA for pattern association

This chapter presents an alternative to the pattern association based on a mixture of local PCA. This mixture is replaced by a single PCA in an infinite-dimensional feature space, into which the data are (virtually) mapped. The principal components in this feature space can be extracted using kernel PCA, which operates only on the data points within the original space (section 2.4). In the original space, a potential field is constructed based on these principal components. To associate an output with an input, a point, whose input portion is given, relaxes along a constraint subspace, whose offset from zero is the input. Herein, relaxation is a gradient descent in the potential field. Potential fields were computed for two-dimensional synthetic data, and the pattern-association method was applied to a synthetic distribution and to the kinematic arm model from section 4.5. On the pattern association, kernel PCA is compared to the mixture of local PCA.

5.1 Motivation

Potential fields are used for pattern association. As for chapter 4, this was motivated by the work of Bachmann et al. (1987) and Dembo and Zeitouni (1988); however, the region of attraction is neither the set of data points nor a set of code-book vectors. Instead, this region is a subspace spanned by principal components (figure 5.1). The problem is that, usually, data are not distributed linearly. A subspace in the original data space would therefore be no good approximation of the data distribution. However, if the data are transformed into a higher-dimensional feature space, the chance is higher that in this space, the image of the data can be separated linearly from the image of its complement (Cover, 1965). Figure 5.2 illustrates this mapping. Thus, we compute the principal subspace in the feature space[1].

---

[1] An alternative might by principal curves and surfaces (Hastie and Stuetzle, 1989). However, kernel PCA has been shown to outperform them (Mika et al., 1999).

In the original space, the potential of a point is given by the square distance of the point's image to this subspace. Images having the same distance lie on a hyper-cylinder (here, defined as the set of points having equal distance to a subspace, for example, in three dimensions and with two principal components, the hyper-cylinder degenerates to two parallel planes). The hyper-cylinder is the iso-potential boundary of a corresponding cylindrical potential field.

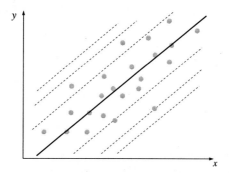

Figure 5.1: The potential increases quadratically when moving in directions orthogonal to the principal subspace (solid line). The dashed lines are iso-potential lines. Gray points are the data distribution.

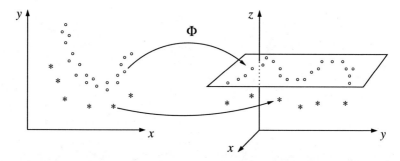

Figure 5.2: Data (∘) are mapped into a higher-dimensional space where they can be linearly separated from points (∗) originating from outside the data distribution. The plane shown is spanned by two principal components.

5.2 Pattern association algorithm

The training data are $\mathbf{x}_i \in \mathbb{R}^d$ with $i = 1, \ldots, n$. In training, the kernel matrix $\tilde{\mathbf{K}}$, its eigenvectors $\mathbf{a}^l$ (section 2.4), and (if used) the reduced set $\{\mathbf{y}_i, \beta_i^l\}$ (appendix B.2) are computed. From these values, the potential E of a point $\mathbf{z} \in \mathbb{R}^d$ can be obtained. In recall, a pattern is completed by a gradient descent in the potential field $E(\mathbf{z})$.

5.2.1 Spherical potential

First, we consider a spherical potential field in feature space. Here, it is not necessary to compute the principal components. All we need is the mean of the data in the feature space,

$$\bar{\varphi} = \frac{1}{n} \sum_{i=1}^{n} \varphi(\mathbf{x}_i) \ . \tag{5.1}$$

The potential of a point $\mathbf{z}$ in the original space is the squared distance from its mapping $\varphi(\mathbf{z})$ to the center $\bar{\varphi}$,

$$E_S(\mathbf{z}) = ||\varphi(\mathbf{z}) - \bar{\varphi}||^2 = \varphi(\mathbf{z})^T \varphi(\mathbf{z}) - 2\,\varphi(\mathbf{z})^T \bar{\varphi} + \bar{\varphi}^T \bar{\varphi} \ . \tag{5.2}$$

Using (5.1), the scalar products can be replaced by the kernel function k (see section 2.4),

$$E_S(\mathbf{z}) = k(\mathbf{z}, \mathbf{z}) - \frac{2}{n} \sum_{i=1}^{n} k(\mathbf{z}, \mathbf{x}_i) + \frac{1}{n^2} \sum_{i,j=1}^{n} k(\mathbf{x}_i, \mathbf{x}_j) \ . \tag{5.3}$$

All parts of this equation are known. The last term is constant, and can therefore be omitted. For radial basis functions (section 2.4.3), the first term is also constant, and the potential can be simplified to:

$$E_S(\mathbf{z}) = -\frac{2}{n} \sum_{i=1}^{n} k(\mathbf{z}, \mathbf{x}_i) \ . \tag{5.4}$$

This function is proportional to the Parzen window density estimator (Parzen, 1962).

5.2.2 Cylindrical potential

We use the reconstruction error (Diamantaras and Kung, 1996, p. 45) as a potential field in feature space,

$$E(\tilde{\varphi}) = \tilde{\varphi}^T \tilde{\varphi} - \tilde{\varphi}^T \mathbf{W}^T \mathbf{W} \tilde{\varphi} \; . \tag{5.5}$$

$\tilde{\varphi}$ is a vector originating in the center of the distribution in feature space, $\tilde{\varphi}(\mathbf{z}) = \varphi(\mathbf{z}) - \bar{\varphi}$. The matrix $\mathbf{W}$ contains the q row vectors $\tilde{\mathbf{w}}^l$ (q is the number of principal components)[2].

We need to eliminate $\tilde{\varphi}$ in (5.5), and write the potential as a function of a vector $\mathbf{z}$ taken from the original space. The projection $f_l(\mathbf{z})$ of $\tilde{\varphi}(\mathbf{z})$ onto the eigenvectors $\tilde{\mathbf{w}}^l = \sum_{i=1}^n \alpha_i^l \tilde{\varphi}(\mathbf{x}_i)$ can be readily evaluated using the kernel function k,

$$
\begin{aligned}
f_l(\mathbf{z}) &= \tilde{\varphi}(\mathbf{z})^T \tilde{\mathbf{w}}^l \\
&= \left[\varphi(\mathbf{z}) - \frac{1}{n} \sum_{r=1}^n \varphi(\mathbf{x}_r) \right]^T \left[\sum_{i=1}^n \alpha_i^l \varphi(\mathbf{x}_i) - \frac{1}{n} \sum_{i,r=1}^n \alpha_i^l \varphi(\mathbf{x}_r) \right] \\
&= \sum_{i=1}^n \alpha_i^l \left[k(\mathbf{z}, \mathbf{x}_i) - \frac{1}{n} \sum_{r=1}^n k(\mathbf{x}_i, \mathbf{x}_r) - \frac{1}{n} \sum_{r=1}^n k(\mathbf{z}, \mathbf{x}_r) \right. \\
&\quad \left. + \frac{1}{n^2} \sum_{r,s=1}^n k(\mathbf{x}_r, \mathbf{x}_s) \right] . \tag{5.6}
\end{aligned}
$$

The second equality uses (5.1). As a result, $E(\mathbf{z})$ can be expressed as

$$E(\mathbf{z}) = \tilde{\varphi}^T \tilde{\varphi} - \sum_{l=1}^q f_l(\mathbf{z})^2 \; . \tag{5.7}$$

The scalar product $\tilde{\varphi}^T \tilde{\varphi}$ equals the potential field of a sphere (5.3). Thus, the expression of the potential $E(\mathbf{z})$ can be further simplified to

$$E(\mathbf{z}) = E_S(\mathbf{z}) - \sum_{l=1}^q f_l(\mathbf{z})^2 \; , \tag{5.8}$$

which is the desired form of the cylindrical potential.

The above computation of $f_l(\mathbf{z})$ requires n evaluations of the kernel function for each $\mathbf{z}$. Since, for each component l, the same kernel can be used, the total number of kernel evaluations is also n. With the speed-up described in appendix B.2, this number can be reduced to m. Here, the expression $\sum_{i=1}^n \alpha_i^l \varphi(\mathbf{x}_i)$ is estimated by $\sum_{i=1}^m \beta_i^l \varphi(\mathbf{y}_i)$, and $1/n \sum_{i=1}^n \varphi(\mathbf{x}_i)$ by $\sum_{i=1}^m \beta_i^0 \varphi(\mathbf{y}_i)$. Doing these replacements, the equation for $f_l(\mathbf{z})$ (5.6) can be approximated by

---

[2]The tilde indicates an eigenvector that belongs to the centered data (section 2.4.2).

$$f_l(\mathbf{z}) = \sum_{i=1}^{m} \left(\beta_i^l - \beta_i^0 \sum_{j=1}^{n} \alpha_j^l \right) k(\mathbf{z}, \mathbf{y}_i)$$

$$- \sum_{i=1}^{m} \sum_{j=1}^{m} \beta_i^0 \beta_j^l k(\mathbf{y}_i, \mathbf{y}_j) + \sum_{r=1}^{n} \alpha_r^l \sum_{i=1}^{m} \sum_{j=1}^{m} \beta_i^l \beta_j^l k(\mathbf{y}_i, \mathbf{y}_j) \; . \quad (5.9)$$

The last two terms and $\sum_{j=1}^{n} \alpha_j^l$ do not need to be evaluated for each $\mathbf{z}$, but can be computed beforehand. Therefore, the computation is dominated by the m evaluations of the kernel function, which need to be carried out only once for all eigenvectors l.

Examples

We study two extreme cases as examples for potential fields. Let σ_d^2 be the maximal variance of the distribution, and σ_f be the size of the smallest structure of interest within the distribution. We use a Gaussian kernel, $k(\mathbf{z}, \mathbf{x}_i) = \exp(-||\mathbf{z} - \mathbf{x}_i||^2/(2\sigma^2))$.

First case, $\sigma \ll \sigma_f$: the kernel function $k(\mathbf{z}, \mathbf{x}_i)$ is almost everywhere approximately zero, apart from $\mathbf{z} \approx \mathbf{x}_i$. Therefore, the spherical potential (5.3) is almost everywhere one, and the projections on the principal components (5.6) are almost everywhere zero. Thus, the potential according to (5.8) is almost everywhere one.

Second case, $\sigma \gg \sigma_d$: the kernel function $k(\mathbf{z}, \mathbf{x}_i)$ is approximately one. If this value is put into (5.3), (5.6), and (5.8) the resulting potential value is zero (for all points).

Both cases do not give desirable potential fields. Therefore, the value of σ should be chosen from the interval $[\sigma_f, \sigma_d]$.

5.2.3 Recall

In recall, the components of a pattern $\mathbf{p}$ are partially given, and the components of a completed pattern $\mathbf{z}$ are divided into input and output (see section 4.2). The input is the offset $\mathbf{p}$ of a hyper-plane extending into the output dimensions:

$$\mathbf{z} = \mathbf{M}\boldsymbol{\eta} + \mathbf{p} \; , \quad (5.10)$$

where $\boldsymbol{\eta}$ are the free parameters of the hyper-plane. The matrix $\mathbf{M}$ defines which dimensions are input and which are output. To obtain the output for a given input, the free parameters are chosen such that the potential $E(\mathbf{z})$ is minimized,

$$\boldsymbol{\eta}^* = \arg\min_{\boldsymbol{\eta}} E(\mathbf{z}(\boldsymbol{\eta})) \ ,$$

$$\mathbf{z}_{\text{opt}} = \mathbf{M}\boldsymbol{\eta}^* + \mathbf{p} \ . \tag{5.11}$$

There seems to be no analytical solution for $\boldsymbol{\eta}^*$. In feature space, the constraint space is not a hyper-plane. However, the minimization can be solved using standard numerical optimization algorithms.

5.3   Experiments

The new pattern-association algorithm is tested on two-dimensional synthetic distributions and on the ten-dimensional kinematic arm model.

5.3.1   Methods

For the tests three synthetic distributions were used, ring-line-square, vortex, and sine-wave, and further data from the kinematic arm model (section 4.5). The ring-line-square distribution is composed of 850 points in a plane. The vortex distribution is also two-dimensional and consists of 700 points. In both sets the points are uniformly distributed in a defined region. The sine-wave is composed of 800 points and is surrounded by 50 outliers (noise). For the kinematic arm model, different from section 4.5, only 5 000 training patterns were generated. Computational limits did not allow a much larger training set ($\mathbf{K}$ is a $n \times n$ matrix).

Kernel PCA was done on all data points of each distribution. A Gaussian kernel with width σ was used. The Gaussian kernel corresponds to a mapping into a countable-infinite-dimensional space (section 2.4.3). Thus, according to Cover's theorem (Cover, 1965), the probability to separate linearly (in feature space) the data distribution from its complement is one. This is favorable. The also commonly used 'polynomial' kernel functions do not have this property (Schölkopf and Smola, 2002). A test with another radial basis function kernel ('inverse multi-quadratic', see section 2.4.3), which also fulfills the above property, showed results similar to those gained from the Gaussian kernel. Therefore, the presentation is restricted to the Gaussian function.

The width σ was set to 0.3 for the ring-line-square, the vortex, and the sine-wave distribution (unless otherwise stated) and to 1.5 for the kinematic arm data. The eigenvectors of $\tilde{\mathbf{K}}$ were extracted using the Power Method with deflation (appendix B.1).

With the speed-up, the potential is computed from a reduced set of m points $\{\mathbf{y}_i\}$ instead of the n data points $\{\mathbf{x}_i\}$ (appendix B.2). To calculate the reduced set, we need to maximize over $\{y_i\}$. Schölkopf et al. (1998a) computed $\{y_i\}$ by iteration. In the present study, however, this was not stable. Sometimes, the iteration ended in an oscillation. Thus, instead, the conjugate gradient method from the Numerical Recipes' code (Press et al., 1993) was used. The values of y_i were initialized randomly within the maximum range of the training data. For all tests, the size m of the reduced set was set to $n/10$.

A quality measure was used to give a quantitative statement on how good a potential field describes the data distribution (appendix B.3). Since we are using uniform distributions, we can define a region that encloses the same volume as the distribution, within an iso-potential curve. The quality is given in percent of the data points covered by that region.

Recall works by solving an optimization problem (see section 5.2.3). The same conjugate gradient method was used to find the parameters $\boldsymbol{\eta}^*$. The components of $\boldsymbol{\eta}$ were initially set to zero.

The recall results were compared to the mixture of PCA (chapter 3 and 4). For training, NGPCA was used. Its parameters were, first, for the sine-wave with noise: $m = 10$ units, $q = 2$ eigenvectors, $t_{max} = 30\,000$, $\rho(0) = 1.0$, $\rho(t_{max}) = 0.001$, $\epsilon(0) = 0.5$, and $\epsilon(t_{max}) = 0.05$, and second, for the kinematic arm data: $m = 100$ units, $q = 6$ eigenvectors, $t_{max} = 400\,000$, $\rho(0) = 10.0$, $\rho(t_{max}) = 0.0001$, $\epsilon(0) = 0.5$, and $\epsilon(t_{max}) = 0.001$ (the same training parameters as in chapter 4).

5.3.2 Results

For the ring-line-square and the vortex distributions, the results compare the spherical with the cylindrical potential field, show the dependence on the two parameters σ and q, and test the performance loss that was due to using a reduced set for speed-up. On the sine-wave distribution and the kinematic arm model, the recall is tested and compared to the mixture of local PCA.

Spherical compared to cylindrical potential

For the ring-line-square distribution, figure 5.3 shows the iso-potential curves of a spherical potential field and a cylindrical potential field with $q = 40$. The 40 principal components explained 94.5% of the variance of the distribution in feature space. The cylindrical field shows a more balanced potential field, having valleys of almost the same depth. This difference is also reflected in the quality measure (93.7% compared to 68.2%).

On the vortex distribution, the cylindrical potential with $q = 40$ could also follow the shape of the distribution better then the spherical field (figure 5.4). The 40 principal components explained 99.0% of the variance.

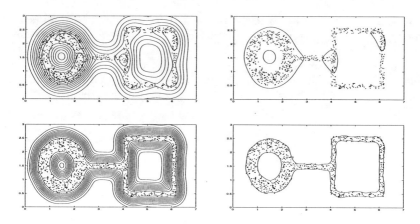

Figure 5.3: Iso-potential curves in the original space of a spherical potential field (top row) and a cylindrical potential field (bottom row) with 40 principal components in feature space. The right pictures show the iso-potential curves enclosing an area of same size as the distribution (top: covering 68.2% of the data points, bottom: covering 93.7% of the data points).

Dependence on the parameters

Kernel PCA depends on the number of principal components q and the width of the Gaussian kernel σ. For the ring-line-square distribution, the quality measure and the fractional variance, explained by the principal subspace in feature space, increased with increasing q (table 5.1). A limit in the quality was reached at about 30 principal components. For 20 principal components, the covered variance also increased with the width σ. However, the quality was almost constant about the tested σ values, with a slight peak at $\sigma = 0.5$ (table 5.2). For the same parameters, the results for the vortex distribution were similar. Here, the optimum was at about $\sigma = 0.1$. The reason for the difference is the smaller variance of the vortex distribution, which requires the optimal σ to be smaller.

Speed-up

Using the speed-up, for the ring-line-square distribution, the potential field based on the reduced set was only sightly impaired (quality: 92.5% compared to 93.7%, compare also figure 5.5 with 5.3). On the vortex distribution, the region surrounded by the iso-potential curve enclosing the same volume as the distribution shows holes (figure 5.5). However, the approximation is still reasonably good (quality: 85.0% compared to 95.0%).

Figure 5.4: Iso-potential curves in the original space of a spherical potential field (top row) and a cylindrical potential field (bottom row) with 40 principal components in feature space. The right pictures show the iso-potential curves enclosing an area of same size as the distribution (top: covering 25.6% of the data points, bottom: covering 95.0% of the data points).

Recall on synthetic data

To test recall, the sine-wave distribution was chosen, which included noise. Thus, this task could also demonstrate the ability to generalize. 15 principal components were extracted (explaining 84.8% of the total variance). The output follows the shape of the sine wave, and it does not get distorted by the outliers (figure 5.6). Here, the right balance of the number of principal components was important. With too many (q=40) extracted components, also the noise was included in the potential field.

The mixture of local PCA could also restore the input-output relationship despite the noise (figure 5.7). Here, all noise points were assigned to one big

Table 5.1: Dependence of the quality Q and variance v—explained by q principal components—on the number of principal components q, for $\sigma = 0.3$ and the ring-line-square distribution.

q	v	Q
10	51.5%	77.1%
20	76.3%	86.5%
30	88.5%	94.2%
40	94.5%	93.7%

Table 5.2: Dependence of the quality Q and the variance v—explained by 20 principal components—on the Gaussian width σ, for the ring-line-square distribution.

σ	v	Q
0.1	25.6%	85.6%
0.3	76.3%	86.5%
0.5	94.3%	87.7%
0.7	98.7%	82.2%

ellipse (in the center of the image). This ellipse did not disturb the recall because the algorithm punishes large ellipsoidal volumes (section 4.2).

Kinematic arm model

The presented potential field method was further applied to the kinematic arm model. Here, 150 eigenvectors were extracted (explaining 67.4% of the total variance), and the reduced set was used. The pattern association based on kernel PCA could learn the inverse one-to-many mapping (table 5.3). However, the association with kernel PCA was worse than with the mixture of local PCA (the position errors were about double). The results were averaged over three separate training cycles. In the table, only averages are shown; the variation was small (for the kernel PCA method the maximum deviation of a position error from a mean value was 2 mm, and for the mixture of local PCA 5 mm).

On this task with fewer training patterns as in section 4.5, NGPCA was restricted to 100 units (in section 4.5, 200 units were used). Increasing this number diminished the performance.

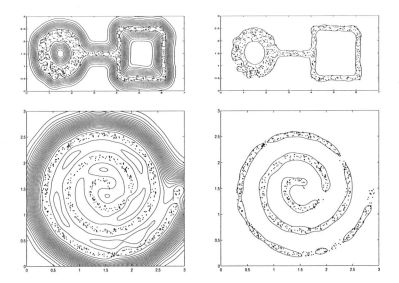

Figure 5.5: Iso-potential curves in the original space of a cylindrical potential field with 40 principal components in feature space. Here, the speed-up as described in section B.2 was used. The right pictures show the iso-potential curve enclosing an area of same size as the distribution (above covering 92.5% and below covering 85.0% of the data points).

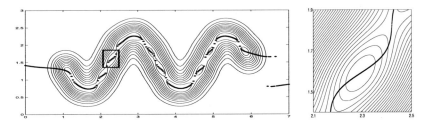

Figure 5.6: Recall in the kernel PCA model trained on a sine wave surrounded by noise (training patterns can be seen in Figure 5.7). The black points show input-output relations. The input is on the x-axis. The right image is a magnification of the region marked with a square in the left image.

5.4 Discussion

A new pattern-association model was introduced. A potential field based on the distribution of training patterns was constructed. In an infinite-

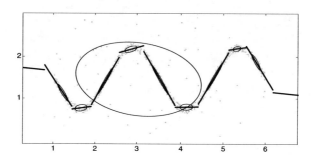

Figure 5.7: Recall in the mixture of PCA model (10 PCAs, with two principal components each). The axes' lengths of the ellipses equal the square root of the eigenvalues. Gray points are the training data. The black lines show input-output relations. The input is on the x-axis.

method	direction	input	position error (mm)	collision error (%)
kernel PCA	inverse	no collision	70 ± 33	2.1
kernel PCA	inverse	collision	75 ± 40	10.2
kernel PCA	forward	—	150 ± 64	20.5
mixture of PCA	inverse	no collision	40 ± 24	7.7
mixture of PCA	inverse	collision	38 ± 27	11.6
mixture of PCA	forward	—	66 ± 46	15.4

Table 5.3: Position and collision errors for an attractor network based on kernel PCA compared to one based on a mixture of local PCA (100 units, $q = 6$). Results are shown for two different directions of recall: forward and inverse. The inverse model takes the desired collision state as an additional input variable (third column). Position errors are averaged over 1331 test patterns, and are given with standard deviations. In the inverse case, the collision error is the percentage of trials deviating from the collision input value; in the forward case, it is the erroneous number of collision state predictions.

dimensional feature space—into which the patterns are virtually mapped—the potential is the squared distanced to a subspace spanned by the principal components. The corresponding field is called cylindrical. Instead of computing in the feature space, the algorithm uses kernel PCA in the original space.

The potential field gained from two-dimensional synthetic distributions resembled accurately the shape of these distributions. Here, the cylindrical potential field in feature space could describe a distribution better than a spherical potential field. The reason is that the cylindrical field accounts for the non-uniform variance in feature space (for ring-line-square, 40 out of 850 principal components described 94.5% of the variance). This comparison also shows that the cylindrical potential field is better than the classical Parzen window density estimator (see section 5.2.1). Given the promising performance on this task, the model could also be applied to novelty detection.

The algorithm needs only two parameters: the number of principal components q and the width σ of the Gaussian kernel. The first gives a control on the complexity of the approximation of the data distribution. In the absence of noise, increasing q increases the quality of the potential field. The number q can be estimated with the help of the amount of variance explained by the principal components; for example, 99% explained variance implies that is it useless to extract more components.

The width σ should be adjusted to about 10% to 50% of the square-root of the total variance of the distribution (the sum over all eigenvalues of the covariance matrix). Small changes seem to have a minor influence on the quality (table 5.2). While for higher σ the principal components explain more of the distribution's variance, the wider Gaussian functions occlude more details.

In recall, the conjugate gradient method was used to minimize the potential field along a subspace whose offset from zero is set by the input to the network. It was demonstrated that the recall algorithm works well on a synthetic distribution, despite the noise in the training set. In contrast, in the models using all training patterns as attractors (Bachmann et al., 1987; Dembo and Zeitouni, 1988), noise points are also attractors, and therefore lead to undesired completions.

The presented relaxation model was further tested on a kinematic arm model. It could cope with the one-to-many mapping (a feed-forward network fails on this task, see section 4.5). The error on the forward mapping was higher (about double) than on the inverse mapping. The reason is possibly the same as discussed in section 4.6.

On the kinematic arm task, the local PCA mixture model did better then the kernel PCA model. The reason might be the multivariate shape of the ellipsoids. In contrast, the kernel PCA model is composed of univariate

Gaussians in the original space (5.6). In the univariate case, many Gaussians might be needed to describe a multivariate structure, which can be described by a single ellipsoid (figure 3.1). The composition of univariate units also results in the sinus-shape-like approximation of a tilted line (figure 5.6, right).

On the kinematic arm data, the mixture model NGPCA was at a limit. With fewer training patterns as in section 4.5, also the number of units needed to be smaller. However, adding more patterns does not necessarily require a longer computation time. In section 4.5, the number of training steps was the same ($t_{\mathrm{max}} = 400\,000$); thus, also the computation times were equal. In contrast, for kernel PCA, increasing the number of patterns n comes at a high cost (the kernel matrix is $n \times n$).

Kernel PCA is computationally demanding. On an Athlon XP 2200+ with 1 GB RAM with a compiled C++ code of the algorithm, the computation of the kernel matrix and the 15 principal components for the sine-wave distribution took about 14 sec. The computation of the reduced set with $m = 85$ took 101 sec, and using the reduced set, the mean recall time was 0.058 sec. In comparison, on the same computer with the same distribution, the mixture model—which was composed of 10 units with two principal components each—had a training time of about 3.7 sec, and a mean recall time of 0.14 msec (about 400 times faster).

The cylindrical potential differs from the square error in the denoising application of kernel PCA (Mika et al., 1999). In denoising of a pattern $\mathbf{x}$, its mapping $\mathbf{\Phi}(\mathbf{x})$ is projected onto the subspace spanned by the principal components in feature space—the same subspace we use for our potential. The denoised pattern $\mathbf{z}$ is obtained by minimizing the squared distance between $\mathbf{\Phi}(\mathbf{z})$ and the projection of $\mathbf{\Phi}(\mathbf{x})$. In contrast, our potential is the squared distance between $\mathbf{\Phi}(\mathbf{z})$ and its own projection onto the subspace. This difference is illustrated in figure 5.8.

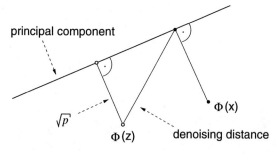

Figure 5.8: Difference between the distance to be optimized in denoising and our potential p.

Kernel PCA requires fewer parameters than a mixture model, but the pattern association based on kernel PCA did worse than the abstract RNN based on a mixture of local PCA. In the next chapter, both methods are applied to visually guided grasping.

Chapter 6

Visuomotor model for a robot arm

The pattern-association methods from chapter 4 and 5 are applied to a robot arm, which is equipped with a camera. An object can be grasped by associating the object's image with an arm posture. Arm postures can be recalled without sensory feedback (open-loop). This enables the robot to perceive (to understand) the position and orientation of an object by associating an appropriate grasping posture and not by mapping the image coordinates to the three-dimensional space. Training data were collected by random exploration. With image preprocessing steps comparable to functions that are known to be performed by the primary visual cortex, the dimensionality of the original images was reduced. On the other hand, the dimensionality of the posture, defined by six joint angles, was increased. This increase improved the performance.

6.1 Visual guided grasping

The robot's task is to reach for and grasp an object that is seen through a camera. The literature on related tasks is briefly reviewed. In the present study, the object is a rectangular shaped brick positioned on a table. Redundant robot arm postures exist to grasp the brick at a given location and orientation. The abstract RNN can cope with this redundancy. However, it cannot associate the arm posture simply from the original image. The high-dimensional image data require preprocessing.

6.1.1 Related work

The presented robot model differs essentially from previous reaching-and-grasping studies. These alternatives differ in at least one of the following three points.

First, some studies work either with reaching or with grasping. For example, Ritter et al. (1989) and Walter et al. (2000) made a robot reach to a point light, which was given in image coordinates. Molina-Vilaplana et al. (2004) also used a point as target. On the other hand, Uno et al. (1995) trained only a robot hand on samples provided by a human equipped with a data glove, and Fuentes and Nelson (1998) manipulated objects that were already in between the gripper.

Second, some studies rely on a representation of the target object in three-dimensional Cartesian space. For example, Cipolla and Hollinghurst (1997) and Molina-Vilaplana et al. (2004) used stereo vision to compute directly the target's coordinates. To compute the target's orientation, Salganicoff et al. (1996) fitted an ellipsoid to three-dimensional data of the target from a laser scanner. Fuentes and Nelson (1998) moved an object with a robot hand by manually providing goal coordinates. Furthermore, like the kinematic arm model in section 4.5, most simulations have as input Cartesian goal coordinates. For example, Oztop et al. (2004), who simulated a human-like arm and hand, used the target's coordinates to compute the arm-joint angles.

Third, some studies operate in closed-loop. Here, the inverse model produces incremental joint-angle changes (Distante et al., 2000; Molina-Vilaplana et al., 2004). Using reinforcement learning, for example, a robot arm can learn to choose the correct reaching direction (Distante et al., 2000).

Closest to our approach is the work by Kuperstein (1988, 1990). His robot can grasp an elongated object in different orientations by mapping visual data onto motor activation that leads to an arm posture. The mapping is carried out by a neural controller. Its training data were gained by sampling randomly the motor space. Different from the abstract RNN, Kuperstein's neural controller is a function from sensory input to motor output and can therefore not cope with one-to-many mappings.

6.1.2   High-dimensional image data

The visuomotor model associates image data with an arm posture. However, the original images cannot be used as part of a training pattern for a mixture of local PCA. Image processing is required, since the dimensionality of the original images is too high and the correlation between neighboring pixels too low. This problem is illustrated in the following example.

A mixture model is trained on images that show an enlongated object that can be grasped. Figure 6.1 displays sample images, which show position and orientation of the object. For simplicity, the images are binary, and the object occupies three pixels. Each image can be written as a vector. Let, E be the squared distance between two image vectors $\mathbf{x}$ and $\mathbf{y}$:

$$E = \sum_i (x_i - y_i)^2 \quad . \tag{6.1}$$

In figure 6.1, the squared distance between **A** and **B** is $E = 6$. The same value holds for all cases in which two images have no overlapping object pixels. These images are in the following called 'disjoint images'. On the other hand, the distance between **A** and **C** is smaller, namely $E = 4$. Thus, rotated objects lie closer to each other than objects at different positions. Two problems result from these facts. First, a density model used to describe the distribution of the disjoint images is meaningless if they all have the same distance to each other. Second, in training, the centers of the mixture model would distribute among disjoint images and average over overlapping images (because of the smaller distance in the second case). Thus, the orientation of the object gets lost. Therefore, the images must be preprocessed.

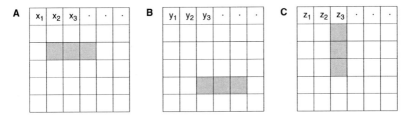

Figure 6.1: Figures **A**, **B**, and **C** show three sample images with corresponding data vectors **x**, **y**, and **z**. White pixels have the value zero, and gray pixels the value one.

6.2 Methods

First, the robot collected samples of images of an object and corresponding grasping postures. Afterward, training patterns were obtained by processing the images and coding the posture angles redundantly using tuning curves. The resulting distribution of patterns was approximated by a mixture of local PCA. After presenting an object, based on the approximation, a grasping posture could be recalled.

6.2.1 Robot setup

The setup was composed of a six-degrees-of-freedom (6 turning joints) robot arm (*Amtec Robotics*) with a linear two-finger gripper and two cameras mounted on a pan-tilt unit (figure 6.3). However, just one camera was used, and its direction was fixed. The camera image was in color and had a resolution of 320×240 pixels. For grasping, a rectangularly shaped ($74 \times 24 \times 24$

mm) red brick was placed on a table in front of the cameras and the arm. The illumination in the room was kept constant.

6.2.2 Data collection

Random exploration was used to collect training data. Initially, the robot arm was in a resting posture, such that it did not occlude the table from the perspective of the camera. Further, the red brick was put in-between the two gripper fingers. One training trial was composed of several steps.

First, a random position on the table (within a 40×30 cm rectangle—its extension on the table can be seen in figure 6.2) and a random orientation ($0°$ to $360°$) were chosen. To make the gripper tip to take this position and orientation, a suitable arm posture was found by solving analytically the inverse kinematics[1].

Figure 6.2: Area of brick positions in the training-data set (view from the left camera). The dark area is the sum over all brick images.

For a given end-effector position and orientation, up to eight solutions of the inverse kinematics exist. At least two solutions exist for any target position, because a $180°$ turn of the joint near the gripper does not have an effect on the grasp. Thus, each image of the brick gives rise to redundant joint-angle sets. For the data collection, one solution was chosen at random.

The resulting arm posture is called a 'grasping' posture. In addition to the position on the table, a second one 60 mm directly above was chosen, and the corresponding joint angles were obtained, as described above. This second posture is called 'pre-grasping' posture (figure 6.3). Both postures were stored.

---

[1]This is a technical shortcut to avoid using a controller that brings the end-effector close to the table surface. The use of the inverse kinematics may be interpreted as an external teacher that guides the arm to random positions on the table.

Figure 6.3: Pre-grasping (left) and grasping posture (right).

In the next step, the robot put the brick on the table. Between two postures, the joint angles were transformed simultaneously and linearly. The arm moved via the pre-grasping to the grasping posture. The use of the pre-grasping posture eases the picking up and putting down of bricks on the table, because collisions with the table and the brick are avoided. These collisions would occur if the arm would turn directly from the resting to the grasping position.

After the brick was put on the table, the arm moved again to the resting position. At this stage, an image from the left camera was taken. Since all brick positions were on a table surface, stereo vision was not necessary. Afterward, the arm repeated the above movement sequence to take back the brick. This concludes one trial. In total, 3371 training patterns and 495 test patterns were collected.

6.2.3 Image processing

The image processing extracts information on the position and on the orientation of the brick (section 6.1.2). The processing consists of several steps:

First, gray-scale images were produced using a contrast mechanism to enhance red $(R - (G + B)/2$, using the RGB-color code). In these images, a rectangle was determined that enclosed the brick in all images (figure 6.4). In the following, only the image region within this rectangle was further processed.

The brick appears almost as a white spot within the contrast image. Thus, a coarse grained version of the image provides a redundant code for the brick's position (figure 6.4). This population code was gained by using a grid of 4 × 4 'neurons' with Gaussian receptive fields. Their centers covered the image uniformly, and the Gaussian width was equal to the distance between two neighboring centers. The resulting 16 activation values were one part of a training pattern. Thanks to the blur in the coarse image, brick locations that were close to each other were also close in the space of the 16 activation values (compare to section 6.1.2).

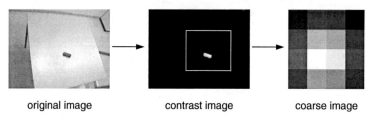

original image   contrast image   coarse image

Figure 6.4: Preprocessing to obtain the position information. The coarse-grained image was gained from the area inside the rectangle in the contrast image.

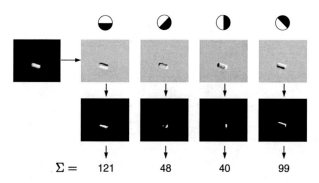

$\Sigma =$ 121   48   40   99

Figure 6.5: Preprocessing to obtain a population code (numbers in bottom row) of the brick's orientation. The first image on the left is the region inside the rectangle within the contrast image in figure 6.4. The columns show the preprocessing steps for each compass filter (top): first, the result of applying the filter, second, the result of applying a threshold, and third, the sum of white pixels in the threshold image.

To obtain a population code for the orientation, the contrast image was first blurred. Then, four compass filters enhanced the edges in four different directions (figure 6.5). To the four resulting images, a threshold function was applied (figure 6.5). The remaining pixels in each image were counted to give a value for the distribution of edges in a given direction (figure 6.5). The result is a histogram showing the edge-direction distribution in the contrast image. Such a histogram can uniquely encode the orientation of the brick at a given location. The four values of this histogram were the second part of a training pattern.

6.2.4 Tuning curves

A training pattern combines visual and postural information. The visual part contains the activation of the 16 Gaussian position neurons and the edge-orientation histogram. Position and orientation were thus represented with a population code.

To obtain also a population code for each joint angle, an angle φ was represented by the activation of four neurons with Gaussian receptive fields, $a_i = \exp(-(\varphi - \varphi_i)^2/(2\sigma^2))$ (using a population code enhanced the performance, see section 6.3). Each of these Gaussians is a tuning curve tuned to the angle φ_i. The Gaussian centers φ_i were uniformly distributed within the maximal range of each angle. The width σ was set equal to the distance between two neighboring centers (figure 6.6).

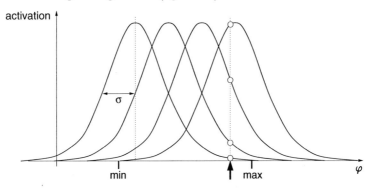

Figure 6.6: A population of four broadly tuned neurons encodes each joint angle φ. The circles show the activations for the angle marked by the thick arrow.

All joint angles of the pre-grasping and the grasping posture were therefore encoded in 48 variables, which form the postural part of a training pattern. The final patterns were thus 68-dimensional. Before training, the patterns were normalized to have unit variance in each dimension. The resulting normalization constants were also applied to the test patterns.

6.2.5   Training

In training, the local PCA mixture models NGPCA, NGPCA-constV, and
MPPCA-ext were used (chapter 3). On the pattern association task, they
were compared to kernel PCA (chapter 5), to a look-up table, and to a multi-
layer perceptron. All of them used the same preprocessed pattern set.

Section 3.3 mentioned that MPPCA-ext comprises the following two modifications: a correction for 'empty' units and the use of an on-line PCA algorithm, which allows that noise can be added to each presented training
pattern. On the visuomotor data, these two modifications turned out to
be essential because otherwise, the algorithm became numerically unstable;
some eigenvalues dropped to zero.

For the mixture models, 120 units and four principal components were
used. The number of principal components was chosen after inspecting the
local dimensionality of the pattern distribution. As described in section 4.5.1,
the ratio of successive eigenvalues, averaged from a PCA in the neighborhood
of each training pattern, has a peak at the local dimensionality of the distribution (Philipona et al., 2003). On the collected data, the first peak is
at three (figure 6.7, left). This matches the expectation, since the brick had
three degrees of freedom: two for the position and one for the orientation.

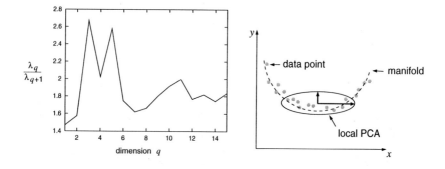

Figure 6.7: (Left) Ratio of successive averaged eigenvalues λ_q and λ_{q+1}. (Right)
Illustration that additional principal components (here, one in y-direction) can
account for the additional variance that results from the manifold's curvature.

Different from the kinematic arm model in section 4.5, however, figure
6.7 shows a second peak at five dimensions. The reason is probably that in
the real robot task, the neighborhood of a pattern also covers the turns and
twists of the underlying manifold because the data are much more sparse
(3371 training patterns lie in a 68-dimensional space, compared to 50 000
patterns in ten dimensions for the kinematic arm model). A turn increases

the local variance (figure 6.7, right). Therefore, for the mixture model, four principal components were chosen instead of three (this also improved the performance).

For NGPCA and NGPCA-constV, two sets of training parameters were used. Set 1 had $\rho(0) = 1.0$, $\rho(t_{\mathrm{max}}) = 0.00001$, $\epsilon(0) = 0.1$, $\epsilon(t_{\mathrm{max}}) = 0.01$, and $t_{\mathrm{max}} = 400\,000$. Set 2 had the same parameters as the kinematic arm model (section 4.5): $\rho(0) = 10.0$, $\rho(t_{\mathrm{max}}) = 0.0001$, $\epsilon(0) = 0.5$, $\epsilon(t_{\mathrm{max}}) = 0.001$, and $t_{\mathrm{max}} = 400\,000$.

Kernel PCA extracted 150 eigenvectors and used an inverse-multiquadratic kernel with width $\sigma = 7.0$ (see section 2.4.3). In the 68-dimensional space, distances are larger than in the previous applications (chapter 5). Thus, the inverse-multiquadratic function was of advantage since it does not decline as quickly as a Gaussian function. Moreover, a reduced set with $m = 1000$ was used (appendix B.2).

The look-up-table method chooses a pattern from the training set whose visual part has the smallest Euclidean distance to the presented input. The multi-layer perceptron maps the visual part to the postural part. A structure with one hidden-layer, containing 20 neurons, was used. The hidden neurons had sigmoid activation functions. The weights were initialized with random values drawn uniformly from the interval $[-0.5; 0.5]$. For training, $3\,000$ epochs of resilient propagation were used (Riedmiller and Braun, 1993).

6.2.6   Recall

In recall, an image from the test set was presented and processed as in section 6.2.3. The resulting 20 dimensional vector defined an offset of a constrained space. Its intersection with the mixture of local PCA provides the output (chapter 4).

Four different methods were compared: the abstract RNN based on a mixture of local PCA, the pattern association based on kernel PCA, the look-up table, and the multi-layer perception. For these methods, the average recall time was measured. All of them were implemented in C++ and were running on an Athlon XP 2200+ with 1 GB RAM.

After recall, each joint angle is given as a population code. Each of the four values φ_i has an activation a_i (section 6.2.4). To obtain the joint angle, a Gaussian function was fitted to the points (φ_i, a_i). Its center equals the desired angle.

With the resulting set of joint-angles, the robot arm is able to grasp the brick by moving from the resting via the pre-grasping to the grasping position. To evaluate off-line the grasping performance on the test set, however, further processing is required. The joints angles were transformed into a gripper position and orientation using a geometric model of the arm (see also section 4.5). The resulting values were compared with the coordinates and orientation of the brick (given in the test set). This comparison gives quantitative errors of position and orientation. Further, a geometric model of gripper tips and brick could determine if the grasping was actually successful. The calculated rate of successful grasps was in agreement with a test on the operating robot (within 1%). Here, the brick was placed 100-times by hand on arbitrary table positions.

6.3 Results

The abstract RNN trained with MPPCA-ext did best at the grasping task, and NGPCA-constV was better then NGPCA (table 6.1). Furthermore, both NGPCA and NGPCA-constV were sensitive to the parameter set. A good performance was only achieved with fine tuned parameters different from the ones used in chapter 4. Kernel PCA could compete with the local PCA mixture models on the grasping performance, but not on the recall speed, which was about 2000-times slower. All of the new methods presented in this thesis were better than a look-up table; the multi-layer perception failed since it cannot cope with redundant arm postures (see also section 4.5).

method	pos. error (mm)	orient. error (degrees)	grasp success (%)	recall time (sec)
MPPCA-ext	7	3.9	95	0.015
$NGPCA_1$	9	4.0	90	0.015
$NGPCA_2$	42	4.9	61	0.015
$NGPCA\text{-}constV_1$	8	4.0	93	0.015
$NGPCA\text{-}constV_2$	26	5.6	77	0.015
kernel PCA	9	4.6	93	31.000
look-up table	13	4.8	87	0.017
MLP	236	54.3	0	< 0.001

Table 6.1: Position error, orientation error, the rate of successful grasps, and the recall time for one trial. The values were averaged over all test trials. The indices for the NGPCA variants refer to the number of the training-parameter set.

Over five different training cycles, the performance of the local PCA mixture models varied only slightly (table 6.2). MPPCA-ext and NGPCA-constV showed less variation compared to NGPCA. The advantage both have over NGPCA is probably also related to the difference in the distribution of assigned patterns per unit (or prior probabilities per unit in the MPPCA-ext case). MPPCA-ext and NGPCA-constV resulted in bell-shaped distribu-

method	position error (mm)	orientation error (degrees)	grasp success (%)
MPPCA-ext	7.3 ± 0.2	3.9 ± 0.2	95.2 ± 0.7
NGPCA	9.1 ± 0.8	4.0 ± 0.4	90.0 ± 1.4
NGPCA-constV	8.0 ± 0.2	4.0 ± 0.2	93.1 ± 0.2

Table 6.2: Average performance over five different training cycles. Standard deviations are given. NGPCA and NGPCA-constV used parameter set 1.

tions; NGPCA resulted in a second peak with 34 units that have less than eight assigned patterns (figure 6.8).

In the presence of noise, the abstract RNN (tested with MPPCA-ext) showed a more robust performance than the look-up table (table 6.3). A second training data set was generated with noise uniformly drawn from the interval $[-0.1; 0.1]$ and added to each component of each pattern. On this set, the number of successful grasps decreased only from 95% to 91% for the abstract RNN; for the look-up table, it decreased from 87% to 57%.

The last test, also using MPPCA-ext, demonstrates the utility of the population code (table 6.4). Two data-processing variants were used. The first had no population codes; each training pattern contained the brick's center of mass in the contrast image, the tilt angle of the main axis of the brick within the image, and the 12 joint angles. Here, despite the reduced dimensionality (15 compared to 68), the number of successful grasps decreased from 95% to 90%. The second variant used the same image processing as in section 6.2.3, but did not encode redundantly the joint angles. This variant decreased the success rate from 90% to 83%.

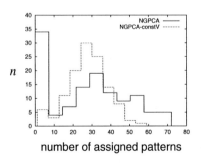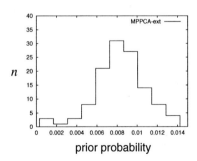

Figure 6.8: Histogram of assigned patterns, respective prior probabilities. n is the number of units for each interval. NGPCA and NGPCA-constV used parameter set 1.

method	position error (mm)	orientation error (degrees)	grasp success (%)
abstract RNN	7.3	3.9	95
abstract RNN, noise	9.0	3.7	91
look-up	13.0	4.8	87
look-up, noise	17.5	5.2	57

Table 6.3: Performance of the abstract RNN (here, using MPPCA-ext) compared to a look-up table. A second training set was used with noise (10% of the standard deviation of the distribution) added to each pattern.

population code	position error (mm)	orientation error (degrees)	grasp success (%)
yes	7.3	3.9	95
no	9.1	2.3	90
only for vision	7.4	14.4	83

Table 6.4: Performance of the abstract RNN with MPPCA-ext using different pattern processing modes (see text).

6.4   Discussion

The abstract recurrent neural network based on the mixture of local PCA and the pattern association based on kernel PCA could both be applied successfully to learn visually guided reaching and grasping. Herein, the recall on the mixture of local PCA was 2000-times faster than on kernel PCA.

MPPCA-ext did better on this task than NGPCA and NGPCA-constV. The distribution of training data is sparse (3371 patterns in 68 dimensions) and thin (locally three-dimensional and little noise). In these cases, MPPCA-ext proved to be better than the NGPCA variants (figure 3.7 and 3.8). NGPCA had problems with dead units (units with no patterns assigned to), see figure 6.8. As expected in section 3.2.1, the modification NGPCA-constV could solve this (figure 6.8). Both NGPCA variants were sensitive to the choice of training parameters (table 6.1).

Reaching and grasping were achieved by associating final arm postures, and not by planning trajectories. This association is consistent with the finding that in the monkey, the stimulation of certain motor cortex neurons leads to hand locations independent of the initial arm posture (Graziano et al., 2002). Moreover, such an association may explain why neurons in the premotor cortex area F5 fire both during the presentation of a tangible object and during the grasping of the object (Rizzolatti et al., 1988; Murata et al., 1997; Rizzolatti and Fadiga, 1998). Murata et al. (1997) wrote, "the visual features are automatically (regardless of any intention to move) 'translated' into a potential motor action" (p. 2229).

The present study further showed that on the one hand, the dimensionality of the original images needs to be reduced, and on the other hand, it cannot be reduced too much; redundancy proved to be helpful. Also in the brain redundancy is widespread. It probably has the following two effects:

First, as mentioned in section 5.1, data points in a higher-dimensional space are more likely to be linearly separable (Cover, 1965). Therefore, they can be better described by locally linear models.

Second, the redundant coding reduces the effect of noise (Latham et al., 2003). The small effect that the noise had on the performance of the abstract RNN (tabel 6.3) can by part be explained with redundancy. The extend of the end-effector positions on the table was 30×40 cm. Thus, without population coding, a 10% noise leads to a position error with variance 208 mm^2 (given a uniform noise distribution). Compared to this value, the increase in the variance of the position error for the look-up table—which cannot use averaging for noise compensation—was smaller ($17.5^2 - 13.0^2 = 137$ mm^2).

For the low performance when using a population code only for the visual information (table 6.4) another explanation was found. Here, the input is 20-dimensional, and the output is only 12-dimensional. In addition, for the same input, redundant postures were possible that only differed in the joint angle near the gripper (section 6.2.2). Thus, the corresponding training patterns differed in only two out of 32 dimensions (one for pre-grasping and one for grasping). Since these patterns were therefore relatively close, they were both assigned to a single unit in the mixture model. Finally, in recall, the output was averaged over the redundant postures within one unit, and this resulted in an erroneous orientation of the gripper. This explains the higher orientation error, while the position error was almost the same as in the case with population coded angles (table 6.4).

The image processing in this chapter relates to biology in several ways. First, it is parallel and local within the image. Second, a compass filter is a simplified version of a simple cell in the primary visual cortex (V1) (Hubel and Wiesel, 1962). Third, like neighboring V1 cells (Blasdel and Salama, 1986), neighboring Gaussian activation functions (coarse image) respond similar to a given stimulus. And fourth, the final preprocessed information is given in population codes.

Population codes and tuning curves are widespread in the brain. Tuning curves can be observed, for example, in the monkey for the direction of moving stimuli (Treue and Trujillo, 1999) and in the cricket for the airflow direction (Miller et al., 1991). The abstract RNN can directly associate one population code with another one, without decoding to scalar values[2]. For the robot arm, the population-coded joint angles were decoded. For a biological system, however, such a step can be omitted since a population code can directly act on a muscle. A theoretical account on this was given by Baldi and Heiligenberg (1988).

The presented robot-arm setup and the flexibility of the abstract RNN offer several options to extend the task: First, the retinal object position (coarse image) can be replaced by information on the gaze direction of the cameras. This was achieved in cooperation with Wolfram Schenck (Schenck et al., 2003). In that study, a saccade controller (Schenck and Möller, 2004) controlled a pan-tilt unit, which supported the stereo camera system. The saccade controller learned to fixate the brick on the table. Then, the tilt and pan variables that define the gaze direction were encoded with tuning curves, as in section 6.2.4. The resulting population codes and the edge histogram were enough to associate an arm posture for grasping. However, the saccade controller required feedback from the environment, and therefore, an understanding of the object's location with covert motor commands is not possible anymore.

Second, monocular vision can be extended to stereo vision. The image processing can be applied to both cameras separately, and the resulting population codes can all be fed into the abstract RNN. Stereo vision would allow grasping in three-dimensional space (Kuperstein, 1990). However, it is difficult to collect training samples because an object held by the robot is at least partially occluded by the gripper.

Third, for grasping, the training set can be extended to bricks that do not lie, but stand on the table. A standing brick can be put on the table with the gripper in a horizontal orientation. Then, the abstract RNN would learn both: lying bricks and standing bricks. As a result, the image of a standing brick would associate a different gripper orientation than the image of a lying brick. The robot could therefore perceive (or understand) if the brick is standing or lying depending on the associated arm posture.

Fourth, the training set can be extended to include other objects. Different objects can be grasped in different ways. The analysis of associated grasping postures could therefore be used to identify the objects[3]. However, this

---

[2]Using an RNN to compute with population codes, instead of extracting the value of the stimulus, was also suggested by Pouget et al. (2003). The authors reviewed computational studies that refer to neuroscience, but did not mention robotics studies.

[3]The model of Uno et al. (1995) recognized objects by associating pictures with prehensile hand shapes using an auto-associative network.

association would not solve object constancy[4], since the association of arm postures cannot do better than a classification of object images. A solution to object constancy could be to anticipate the sensory consequence of a sequence of motor commands (section 1.4.3, (Möller, 1999)). Chapter 7 presents a mobile robot that simulates such a sequence.

---

[4]Object constancy means that an object can be recognized independently of the perspective and the illumination.

Chapter 7

Forward model for a mobile robot

This chapter investigates whether both planning goal-directed movements and judging the geometry of the surroundings can be based on a forward model (Hoffmann and Möller, 2004). Tests were done with a mobile robot, which was equipped with a camera. A forward model was put into effect either as a multi-layer perceptron (MLP) or as an abstract recurrent neural network (RNN). The robot collected training data by random exploration. A training pattern for the forward model was obtained from two successive images and the corresponding motor commands. To predict the sensory consequence of a sequence of motor commands, multiple copies of the trained forward model can be linked to a chain. On this prediction, a chain of MLP was more accurate than a chain of abstract RNNs. For goal-directed movement planning, an optimization method yielded the required motor commands. For judging the geometry of the surroundings, the simulation of covert motor commands revealed the connection between self-motion and sensory input.

7.1 Introduction

This chapter connects to the concept of perception being based on sensorimotor models, as described in section 1.4.3. Several tasks serve as an illustration of the principle.

7.1.1 Motivation

The demonstration has mainly two purposes: First, it shall show that a forward model can serve as a building block that allows to use simulation either for planning actions or for perceiving space. Such an approach does not need a world representation based on a coordinate frame, or any one-to-one mapping from the world to an internal representation (Möller, 1999; Jirenhed et al., 2001; Hesslow, 2002; Grush, 2004).

Second, the demonstration shall show *how* the mastery of sensorimotor relations, which is proposed by Möller (1999) and O'Regan and Noë (2001) to be the basis of visual perception, might lead to an understanding of the geometry of the surrounding (section 1.4.3). In particular, in one task, it is shown that this mastery can take advantage of the spatial symmetry. Thus, symmetry can be perceived (detected) without having a sensory representation that reflects this symmetry, as in the thought experiment with the perception of a straight line (O'Regan and Noë, 2001), see section 1.4.3.

7.1.2   Tasks

In all experiments, the robot was located inside a circle of obstacles. First, the robot collected training data by randomly choosing wheel velocities and taking images through his omni-directional camera in intervals of two seconds. Then, each image was processed to obtain a lower-dimensional sensory representation. On two successive sensory representations and corresponding wheel velocities, a forward model was acquired either by using an MLP or by using the abstract RNN (chapter 4).

A single forward model can predict the future sensory input S_{t+1} after a two second interval given the current sensory input S_t and the current wheel velocities M_t. In a chain of forward models, the sensory output at link t is feed into the sensory input at link $t + 1$. Thus, the chain can anticipate the sensory consequence of a series of motor commands.

In a first test, the anticipation performance was evaluated on a separate test set that contains random movement sequences. The changes in prediction error with an increasing number of prediction steps are analyzed for the multi-layer perceptron, the abstract RNN, and compared to a theory of the error accumulation (appendix C.3).

In the first task, the forward-model chain was applied to find a series of velocity commands that makes the robot reach a goal state. The goal state was defined within the sensory domain. The difference between the goal state and the final predicted sensory state defined a cost function. By minimizing this cost function, using either simulated annealing or Powell's method (Press et al., 1993), an appropriate series of velocities was found.

In the second task, the robot had to detect whether it was standing in the center of the circle or not. The robot could solve this task by simulating a turn around its rotational axis and by predicting the resulting sensory input. Because of the match between the robot's rotational axis and the symmetry axis of the world, the invariance in time of the predicted sensory state reflects the spatial invariance in the world.

In the third task, the robot had to judge the relative distance to obstacles, despite the non-linear mapping from the world to the camera image. This was also achieved by mental transformation. Here, a forward movement was simulated. The number of simulated movement intervals that were needed to reach the obstacle in front was counted. This number served as an estimate of the relative distance to an obstacle. Thus, the robot can perceive the real geometric relations, which are a priori not accessible to a pure sensory representation. Mallot et al. (1992, p. 16) also mentioned the possibility that distance can be perceived as 'time-to-contact'.

7.2 Methods

This section describes the robot setup, the data collection by random exploration, the image processing, the acquiring of a forward model with a multi-layer perceptron and with an abstract recurrent neural network, and the methods for the two basic task sets: goal-directed movement planning and mental transformation.

7.2.1 Robot setup

A *Pioneer 2 AT* four-wheel robot from *ActivMedia Robotics* was used (see figure 7.1, left). It has differential steering and was equipped with a panoramic vision system based on an omni-directional hyperbolic mirror ('middle size, wide view') from *Accowle* (figure 7.1, right)[1]. The camera's optical axis was positioned 12 cm in front of the robot's rotational axis. Images were grabbed at a resolution of 640 × 480 pixels. A circularly shaped cover on top of the mirror prevented light entering directly into the lens without reflexion from the mirror. The illumination of the room was kept constant during training and tests.

7.2.2 Data collection

Training and test data were collected using two different random exploration schemes.

Training data

The training data contain series of images induced by given motor commands. The robot was put within a circle with an inner diameter of 180±2 cm formed by red bricks (figure 7.1, left).

---

[1]A DFK 4303/P camera and a Pentax TS2V314A lens were used.

Figure 7.1: (Left) Pioneer robot with omni-directional camera surrounded by 15 red obstacles. (Right) Panoramic vision system.

Random velocities were chosen for the left and right wheels individually (v_L and v_R). The velocities ranged from -60 mm/sec to 60 mm/sec in steps of 20 mm/sec. The combination with both velocities being zero was discarded.

After a set of velocities was chosen, the robot maintained the given speed. Every two seconds, an image was recorded from the camera (figure 7.3, left) and stored. Recording started after granting the robot a one second acceleration phase. The movement lasted up to a maximum of six shots (five 2 sec intervals) or until the robot got too close to one of the obstacles (this was determined with the help of the same kind of image preprocessing as described in section 7.2.3). In both cases, a new combination of velocities was chosen, and a new recording series started.

In the second case, however, the choice of velocities was restricted. The robot was only allowed to go either forward or backward, depending on if the obstacle was in the back or front. Forward movements were chosen randomly from a subset that fulfills $v_L v_R \geq 0$ and $v_L + v_R > 0$. Backward movements were chosen in an analogue way ($v_L v_R \geq 0$ and $v_L + v_R < 0$).

This data-collection scheme would result in more forward and backward movements against rotational movements (which fulfill $v_L v_R < 0$) because the robot was not allowed to do turns when it was close to obstacles. Therefore, when a rotation was possible, the rotational movements were chosen with a higher probability to adjust toward a balanced distribution of velocity combinations.

The actual wheel velocity was recorded during the 2 sec intervals. If it deviated by more than 10 mm/sec from the given value the series was stopped, and the interval's was data discarded. After that, a new series started, as above. The robot was able to pursue this kind of random exploration automatically without getting into physical contact with any obstacle.

In total, 5466 intervals with 6808 images were recorded. The velocities were roughly evenly distributed (figure 7.2). Straight movements ($v_L = v_R$) slightly dominated, and there were fewer slow turns like $v_L = 0$ and $v_R = 20$ mm/sec. The explanation is that the lateral friction between wheels and floor made the robot occasionally stick to the ground during slow turns, so these movements were discarded.

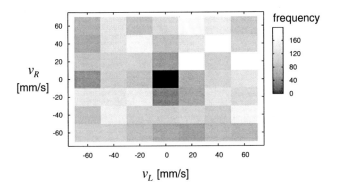

Figure 7.2: Distribution of velocities v_L and v_R.

Test data

For an off-line evaluation of the anticipation performance, test data were collected using a slightly different random exploration scheme. The goal was to get random movement sequences instead of series with a constant motor command.

For each interval, a new random velocity combination was used. A recording series consisted of eight 2 sec intervals starting from zero velocity. The first interval was discarded, thus leaving seven intervals each under identical conditions. The wheel velocity was monitored in the last 0.7 sec of each interval. If its mean value deviated by more then 10 mm/sec from the given value the whole recording series was discarded. Therefore, the limited acceleration required to make the random choice of velocities slightly dependent on the previous choice. Absolute velocity changes of more than 60 mm/sec for each wheel were not allowed.

The choice of velocities in each interval further depends on the encounters with obstacles. If the obstacle was in the front the robot moved backward, and if it was in the back the robot moved forward (same way as done for the training data). Additionally, the robot responded to an obstacle on the left or right side by turning the front of the robot toward the obstacle (choosing $|v_L| > |v_R|$, $v_L > 0$, and $v_R < 0$ for obstacles on the right side, and accordingly for the left side, changing roles of v_L and v_R). The turn toward the obstacle was then followed by a backward movement.

Such a response to the obstacles allowed the rear part of the robot to keep a larger distance to the circle. This was necessary since the mirror was located in the frontal part of the robot (see figure 7.1), and thus the bottom part of an obstacle close to the rear part of the robot was occluded. Totally, 138 test series were recorded, with a total of 966 intervals and 1104 images.

7.2.3   Image processing

It proved to be impossible to use the original visual information in the training for the following reasons. First, the dimensionality is too high, and second, the color of single pixels may alter drastically even for small changes in the robot's location. If each pixel value would represent a single dimension, the jumps in sensorimotor space would be too large for any function approximation. Therefore, the image was preprocessed to detect only a special class of objects and extract only a visual distance information in a few sectors. Image processing contained the following steps:

First, a contrast mechanism enhanced red objects $(R - (G + B)/2)$. The result was smoothened with a binomial filter. Then, a threshold function was applied on all pixel values (figure 7.3, right). Within the obtained binary image, in ten sectors (36° each), the distance from the center of the robot to the closest object was determined (figure 7.3, right). These ten distance values form the final representation of the sensory input to be processed by the network (figure 7.4). Such a sensory representation in sector values was also used by Tani (1996). Different from our model, he used a laser sensor instead of vision.

The 'motor commands' v_L and v_R together with two corresponding image representations (as in figure 7.4) from two consecutive recordings (2 sec apart) make one training pattern. Each pattern is therefore a 22-dimensional vector. Before network training, the set of training patterns was normalized to have zero mean and unit variance in each dimension. The resulting normalization constants were also applied to the test set and the robot experiments.

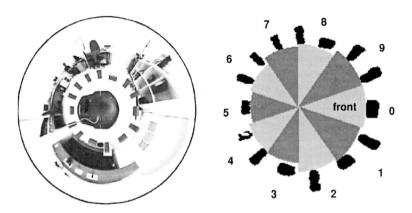

Figure 7.3: (Left) Image as seen through the mirror. (Right) Distance information in ten sectors derived from the image on the left.

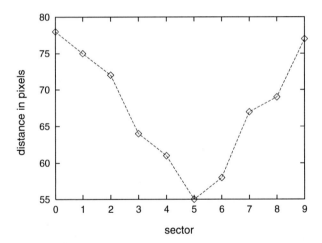

Figure 7.4: Visual distance in ten sectors for the situation in figure 7.3.

7.2.4 Forward model: Multi-layer perceptron

All tasks in this chapter depend on a forward model. It gets as input the sensory information (figure 7.4) of one time step and the motor command consisting of the velocities v_L and v_R, and it predicts the sensory information of the next time step. Training data were collected as described in section 7.2.2.

To anticipate future sensory information beyond the 2 sec prediction horizon of a single forward model, we feed the sensory output back into the sensory input (figure 7.5). This feedback completely overwrites the previous input. At each time step t, the corresponding motor command M_t (here, velocity combinations) of the sequence is fed into the network. Thus, for illustration it seems more intuitive to replace the feedback by a chain of identical forward models (figure 7.6).

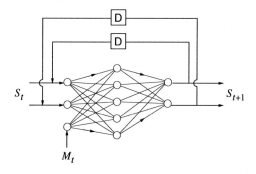

Figure 7.5: Forward model with feedback loop. The model maps the sensory information S_t onto S_{t+1} in the context of the motor command M_t. The boxes labeled D delay the feedback by one time step.

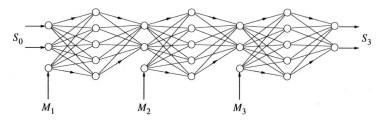

Figure 7.6: Concatenated chain of forward models. The sensory output of link t is the sensory input of link $t+1$.

First, as a forward model, an MLP with one hidden layer was used. The network's activation functions were the identity on input and output layer, and the sigmoidal function in the hidden layer. The MLP had 12 input neurons (two velocity values and the ten sector values) and ten output neurons (ten sector values). The hidden layer comprises 15 hidden units. This number seemed to be a good compromise between recall speed and accuracy. Higher numbers did not improve the performance noticeably. The weights were initialized with random values drawn uniformly from the interval $[-0.5; 0.5]$. The network was trained on 5466 patterns with 3000 epochs of resilient propagation (RPROP) (Riedmiller and Braun, 1993). The performance of the MLP is shown in section 7.3.1.

7.2.5 Forward model: Abstract recurrent neural network

The abstract RNN was used as an alternative to the MLP. Tests were carried out on two data sets, called 'standard' and 'change'. The first is the same as for the MLP. In the second set, the predicted sensory state S_{t+1} is replaced by the relative change $\Delta S_t = S_{t+1} - S_t$. Thus, the network output needs to be added to the current sensory state to obtain the predicted state.

For the training, MPPCA-ext, NGPCA, and NGPCA-constV were used (chapter 3). The number of units was 50. NGPCA and NGPCA-constV had the same training parameters as in chapter 4, namely $\rho(0) = 10.0$, $\rho(t_{max}) = 0.0001$, $\epsilon(0) = 0.5$, $\epsilon(t_{max}) = 0.001$, and $t_{max} = 400\,000$.

To get an estimate of the number q of principal components needed for each training set, the local dimensionality of the pattern distribution was computed. This was done as in section 4.5. The peak in the ratio of successive averaged eigenvalues—from a local PCA within the neighborhood of each training pattern—was determined. Here, the number of neighbors differed from the one given in section 4.5. This number needs to be sufficiently large to point out the underlying dimensionality (figure 7.7, left). For the standard set, the peak in the eigenvalue ratio is at four (figure 7.7, left). As expected, the robot's location (distance from the circle center), its orientation, and the two velocities make four degrees of freedom. For the change set, however, this peak was at 13 (figure 7.7, right). Here, the explanation is that the noise-to-signal ratio is higher; the noise in ΔS_t equals about the noise in S_t, but the magnitude of ΔS_t is about ten-times smaller than the magnitude of S_t. The additional variance increases the local dimensionality.

The mixture models were tested with $q = 5$ for the standard set and with $q = 14$ for the change set. As in section 6.2.5, one principal component was added to take care of the curvature of the distribution. This improved the performance.

As shown in chapter 4, the abstract RNN can associate patterns in any direction; the MLP is restricted to the trained direction. To demonstrate this advantage of the RNN, another experiment used the same trained RNN as an inverse model. Here, two successive states S_t and S_{t+1} are mapped onto the motor command M_t. The performance of the abstract RNN is shown in section 7.3.2.

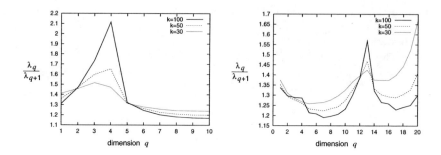

Figure 7.7: Ratio of successive averaged eigenvalues λ_q and λ_{q+1}. For different numbers k of neighbors, results are shown for the standard training set (left) and the change set (right).

7.2.6   Performance outside the training domain

Both the abstract RNN and the MLP were only trained on data points whose sensory components were restricted to a two-dimensional manifold. The free parameters are the robot's distance to the center of the circle and the robot's orientation. Since it is not clear how a network reacts to points slightly outside its training domain, we have a look at the effect of a small change in the input of the forward model.

Let $\mathbf{f(s)}$ be the transformation the network does on the sensory input. To each sensory input $\mathbf{s}$ from the test set, in ten trials, a divergence $\mathbf{e}$ was added. This divergence was distributed randomly and extended uniformly into the ten-dimensional sensory subspace. The magnitude of $\mathbf{e}$ ranged between 0.0 and 1.0 pixels. The computation of $\mathbf{f(s)}$ also requires a pair of velocities; in each trial, they were chosen randomly from the interval [-60; 60]. The results are in section 7.3.3.

7.2.7   Anticipation performance

To test the anticipation performance, a separate set was used (section 7.2.2). The reason is that a theoretical prediction of the dependence of the anticipation error on the chain length relies on randomly independent errors for each prediction step (appendix C.3). Randomly independent errors are unlikely for series with a constant motor command. Therefore, the test patterns were collected during random walks.

However, the slight dependence of velocities, as mentioned in section 7.2.2, results in a deviation from a pure random walk. As the dashed curve in figure 7.8 indicates, the square distance (in the sensory representation) to the starting point of a sequence increases stronger than linear, which would be the expectation for a random walk (appendix C.3). In addition, the limited movement range within the circle of obstacles reduced the increase of the square distance for longer sequences. Still, for intermediate sequence lengths, the increase is roughly linear (figure 7.8, solid line). Therefore, for the comparison with the theory, and to compute the average linear increase of the square error, only the prediction intervals 2 to 6 were evaluated.

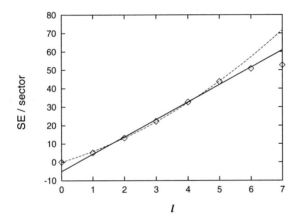

Figure 7.8: Increase of the mean squared distance per image sector (in pixels squared) from the sensory representation after interval l to the representation at the starting point of a sequence. The dashed curve is a quadratic function fitted to the intervals zero to five. The solid line shows the almost linear increase between interval one and six.

The square error E^2 of the anticipation was evaluated after each chain link l. The error E^2 is the squared difference between the output **o** of a chain with l links and the real sensory information **r** after l 2 sec intervals,

$$E^2 = \sum_{i=1}^{10}(o_i - r_i)^2 \ . \tag{7.1}$$

7.2.8 Goal-directed movements

The task in the planning of goal-directed movements is to find a series of motor commands such that the final sensory information matches the desired value. Here, this problem is treated as an optimization task. The function to be optimized is the square error between anticipated and desired goal.

In our experiments, the goal state was not the complete sensory information, as in (7.1), but only the value g_i in a predefined sector i. Thus, the cost
function is $E^2 = (o_i - g_i)^2$, with o_i equal to the predicted output in sector i.
First, we assume that we know the appropriate number of chain links. The
free parameters are the velocities v_L and v_R for each time step (link in the
chain).

Two different optimization methods were applied, simulated annealing
and Powell's method from the 'Numerical Recipes' (Press et al., 1993). The
first is more suited to find a global minimum, whereas the second might be
caught in a local minimum.

Simulated annealing is a stochastic method for minimum search, occasionally allowing jumps to higher values of the cost function. The probability
of these jumps is given by the Boltzmann distribution. The temperature
parameter of this distribution is slowly reduced during the simulation, according to an annealing scheme. In the present study, a variant (Carter Jr.,
1994) of the 'Fast Simulated Annealing' (Szu and Hartley, 1987) was used.
This variant starts with increasing the temperature up to a point at which a
large jump to a higher value in the cost function occurs, and then decreases
the temperature. The default parameters from Carter Jr. (1994) were used,
except for the learning rate, which was set to 0.1, and the number of random
steps at each temperature value, which was set to 20 times the number of
free parameters. Random numbers were generated using the algorithm 'ran1'
from the Numerical Recipes (Press et al., 1993).

Powell's method is based on conjugate directions, but does not need the
evaluation of a gradient. Here, the parameters were taken from the Numerical
Recipes (Press et al., 1993). The fractional tolerance of the cost function
was set to 10^{-4}. Both optimization methods were initialized by setting all
velocities to zero.

The treatment of the goal-directed movement as an optimization problem
allows us to add penalty terms to the square error to restrict the possible
range of solutions. The choice of velocities beyond the range ± 60 mm/sec,
used for training, was prohibited by punishing velocities outside this range
with an additional term in the cost function ($+10\,000$ pixels squared). This
term was necessary because otherwise, for goals out of the reach of one interval, the optimization could result in large velocities for which no examples
were available in the training set (for these velocities, the extrapolation of
sensory predictions found by the network may be incorrect). To avoid collisions, a penalty term ($+100$ pixels squared) was added to velocity series that
result in robot positions too close to an obstacle.

So far, we have assumed that the number of chain links is given; however,
the number of time steps required to achieve a goal is not known beforehand.
Therefore, we start with one link and increase the number of links in the

optimization process. For each number of links, we solve the optimization and test if the resulting state matches the desired state (within 0.5 pixels— the resolution limit). If this criterion is not yet met, the number of links is increased by one and the optimization restarts from zero velocities. This is repeated until the criterion is met.

To test the goal-directed movements quantitatively, a random series of goals was chosen. A trial consisted of choosing a goal and executing the resulting movement. The goal sector was chosen among the ten sectors, and its value was chosen from the interval $[50, 65]$. With the given shape of the robot and the arrangement of the obstacles, it was physically possible for each sector to attain these values. At the beginning of each trial, an image was taken, which was used as the starting point of the anticipation. At the end of a trial, another image was taken for comparison with the desired goal. In the next trial, the robot started from where it ended in the previous movement sequence. The robot did two blocks of 50 trials. At the beginning of each block the robot was placed in the middle of the circle. This was done to increase the variety of movements, because at the end of a block, the robot happened to spend most of its time near the obstacles. The results are in section 7.3.4.

7.2.9 Mental transformation

Two mental transformations were carried out: a simulated rotation around the robots axis, and a simulated translation toward the barrier of obstacles. In the first, the robot has to estimate whether it is standing in the center of the circle. In the second, the robot has to estimate the distance to the obstacle in front.

In figure 7.3, the robot is roughly in the middle of the circle, but apparently this cannot be decided from the image representation (figure 7.4). The reason for this asymmetry is that the center of the robot differs from the optical axis of the camera. However, the location can be estimated by simulating a turn around the rotational axis of the robot and by predicting the distance in the frontal sector.

After observing the current image, the robot simulated a left and a right turn (around its rotational axis, i.e., $v_L = -v_R$), and anticipated the effect of these movements on the image representation. From the current position the robot simulated five rotational steps (2 sec each) to the left with the velocity $v_L = -40$ mm/sec and $v_R = 40$ mm/sec, and, also from the current position, five steps to the right at the opposite velocity. Five steps at this speed corresponded to a rotation of $72°$. Since the obstacles were standing in a circle, it was not necessary to cover the entire $360°$ in the mental simulation. Then, the values of the frontal sector for the different representations were compared (altogether 11 values). If they had a variance of less than one pixel squared it was concluded that they were the same, and thus the robot centered in the circle (which is the only point having same distance to the circle boundary in all directions). 20 trials were evaluated, with the robot placed at 20 arbitrary positions (in the vicinity of the center) with random orientation.

In the second task, the robot simulated a forward movement at speed $v = 40$ mm/sec. The frontal sector value was predicted. If it dropped below a threshold, the simulation stopped. The threshold was chosen such that the bottom part of the obstacle was still just visible and not occluded by the robot body. The robot was placed at 15 arbitrary positions on a line through the center of the circle. The distance between the forefront of the robot and the forefront of the obstacle in front was measured. The results of these two tasks are in section 7.3.5.

7.3   Results

First, on the test data, this section shows the anticipation performance for the MLP and for the abstract RNN and an analysis of predictions from outside the training domain. Second, on the robot, the MLP chain is applied to goal-directed action-selection and mental transformation.

7.3.1   Anticipation with the multi-layer perceptron

For the multi-layer perceptron, the average error on the 138 test pattern series is shown in figure 7.9. The mean square error was below 2.4 pixels squared for all tested chain lengths. Starting from the second to the sixth step the square error per sector increases linearly. This linear increase matches the theoretical prediction (appendix C.3).

7.3.2   Anticipation with the abstract recurrent neural network

For the abstract recurrent neural network, the error increase over time was worse than for the MLP (table 7.1 and 7.2). On the standard training set, MPPCA-ext was better than NGPCA and NGPCA-constV for the anticipated q value of 5 (table 7.1). With a larger q value, however, the performance of NGPCA and NGPCA-constV increased, while it decreased for MPPCA-ext.

On the change set, NGPCA-constV did better than the other two methods (table 7.2). Here, the distributions of assigned patterns (respective prior probabilities) differed clearly (figure 7.10). In the NGPCA-constV case, the

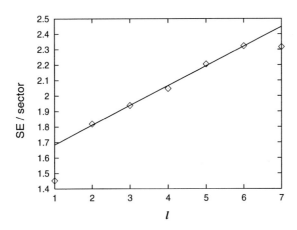

Figure 7.9: Anticipation performance of the MLP on the 138 test series. The mean square error (in pixels squared) per sector is shown as a function of the number l of chain links. A line is fitted to the points from link number two to six.

distribution is confined to a smaller range of numbers compared to the two other cases. Moreover, NGPCA results in 13 units with only a few assigned patterns (less than 30). The test with the change set further shows that more principal components were needed than in the standard case to achieve an almost equal performance (table 7.2).

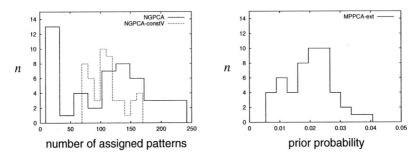

Figure 7.10: Histogram of assigned patterns, respective prior probabilities. n is the number of units for each interval. Here, the change set and 14 principal components were used.

The abstract RNN can also learn the inverse direction from two successive sensory states to the two wheel velocities (table 7.1 and 7.2). However, the error is too high for robot control. The square root of the square error is around 20% of the total velocity range. This error is actually so large that the prediction of motor commands can only be used to determine if the robot goes forward or backward, or turns left or right, as a function of the alternating camera image.

method	q	1-step error (pixel^2)	error increase (pixel^2)	inv. dir. error (mm/sec)
MPPCA-ext	5	1.8	0.30	27
NGPCA	5	1.7	0.46	25
NGPCA-constV	5	1.8	0.52	27
MPPCA-ext	7	1.8	0.39	25
NGPCA	7	1.7	0.30	24
NGPCA-constV	7	1.7	0.30	24
MLP	-	1.5	0.13	-

Table 7.1: Anticipation performance (on the 138 test series) of the abstract RNN trained on the standard set. The results for the multi-layer perceptron are shown for comparison. q is the number of principal components. The *1-step error* is the average square error per sector for the first predicted interval. The *error increase* is the average square error increase per sector and interval between the second and the sixth interval (obtained by a linear fit as in figure 7.9). For the inverse direction, the last column shows the square-root of the average square error of the predicted velocity.

method	q	1-step error (pixel^2)	error increase (pixel^2)	inv. dir. error (mm/sec)
MPPCA-ext	14	1.8	0.46	23
NGPCA	14	2.0	0.81	22
NGPCA-constV	14	1.6	0.28	23
MPPCA-ext	7	1.9	0.51	24
NGPCA	7	1.9	0.77	24
NGPCA-constV	7	1.8	0.45	24
MLP	-	1.4	0.20	-

Table 7.2: Anticipation performance (on the 138 test series) of the abstract RNN trained on the change set. The results for the multi-layer perceptron are shown for comparison. See table 7.1 for further explanation.

The main difference in the performance between the abstract RNN and the MLP is the difference in the linear square error increase. The best obtained value for the abstract RNN of 0.28 pixels squared per interval (table 7.2) is more than double than the best MLP value of 0.13 pixels squared (table 7.1). Furthermore, compared to the MLP, the abstract RNN was not only less accurate in the forward prediction, but also slower. On an Athlon 2200+ with 1GB RAM, a single mapping with the abstract RNN took 1.3 ms and with the MLP 0.016 ms (both algorithms were implemented in C++). Thus, for the applications of the chain, only the MLP was used.

7.3.3 Performance outside the training domain

For both abstract RNN and MLP, in contrast to the prediction (appendix C.3), the error increase per interval was smaller than the error for one predicted step. To investigate the cause, we first study how the forward models perform on points outside the training domain.

Figure 7.11 shows the change of the forward-model output, $\mathbf{f}(\mathbf{s}+\mathbf{e}) - \mathbf{f}(\mathbf{s})$, as a result of a small divergence $\mathbf{e}$ from a given sensory input from the test set. In the MLP case, the major part of the change in the output is concentrated around a line with slope 0.5. Thus, sensory states outside the training domain were mapped back, closer to the domain. In the abstract RNN case, this also holds for most of the test points. However, some points were mapped further away from the domain (top part in figure 7.11, right).

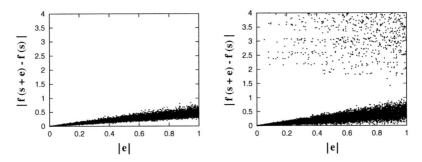

Figure 7.11: Response of the forward mapping $\mathbf{f}(\mathbf{s})$ to small deviations $\mathbf{e}$ from a test pattern input $\mathbf{s}$, for the MLP (left) and for the abstract RNN (right). All values are in pixels. The abstract RNN was trained on the standard set with MPPCA-ext and $q = 5$. The right diagram is typical for all tested mixture models.

The sensory input from the training and test data is restricted to a two-dimensional manifold. Thus, a single prediction steps starts from this manifold, and its error can extend into all ten directions. In a sequence, however, the sensory input for some steps has left the manifold. In these cases, as shown in the experiment, the sensory state is mapped back toward the manifold. Therefore, the directions the error can go are restricted to the directions within the manifold. Thus, different from the assumption in appendix C.3, the sequence of errors did a random walk in two dimensions instead of ten. This led to more error compensations and thus to a slower error increase.

To test this argument further, the square error between successive prediction steps was compared. In accordance with the argument, the observed percentage of error compensations was 45% for the MLP and around 40% for the abstract RNN (this percentage is higher than for a random walk in ten dimensions).

7.3.4   Goal-directed movements

The goal for the robot is to move in a way that the sensory value in a single given sector reaches a given value. Figure 7.12 illustrates the result of two typical movements. In example A, the goal was to make the sector in the back right (number 4 in figure 7.3, right) attain a low value (for example, 50 pixels). The robot moved backward in a rightward curve. In example B, the front sector should attain a low value. Thus, the robot moved from the middle of the circle straight toward the obstacles.

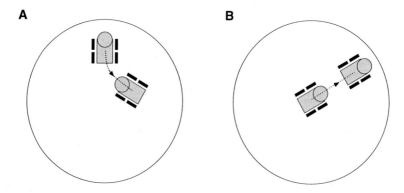

Figure 7.12: Typical goal-directed movements. The goal was to be close to an obstacle (A) in the back right sector (number 4 in figure 7.3) or (B) in the front sector (number 0 in figure 7.3).

The two optimization methods gave similar results (table 7.3). In almost all trials, both optimization methods found a solution (96% to 99%). In

15% to 18% of the trials, the final sector value matched exactly the desired value, and in almost half of the trials, the final value was within one pixel of the desired value. In more than 80% of the trials, the final sector value was closer to the desired than to the initial value, and in more than 90% of trials, the final sector value was changed in the right direction (increasing or decreasing).

	sim. anneal.	Powell
found solution	99%	96%
exact hits	18%	15%
close within one pixel	41%	46%
closer to goal	85%	83%
right direction	91%	91%
mean square error/link	4.4	2.6
mean number of links	2.8	2.5

Table 7.3: Result of 100 goal-directed movements for simulated annealing and Powell's method.

The almost equal performance of the Simulated Annealing and the Powell's method did not depend on choosing just one goal sector. No noticeable difference was also observed when two and three defined goal sectors were defined (data not shown).

7.3.5 Mental transformation

Using mental transformation, the robot could determine whether it was standing in the middle of the circle (figure 7.13), and it could determine the distance to the obstacle in front (figure 7.14).

On the first test, figure 7.13 shows which locations were classified as being in the center and which not. Among the positions that were classified as center, the maximum distance to the center was 10 cm.

On the second test, the number of predicted steps toward the obstacles scaled with the real distance (figure 7.14). A line was fitted to the data. In all trials, the deviation from the line was less then one step. From the slope of the line the speed of the simulated movement can be estimated. The slope is 6.6 ± 0.2 cm/step and corresponds to a speed of 33 ± 1 mm/sec (the actual speed for the given velocity command was 33.5 mm/sec: 40mm/sec divided by a conversion factor for the wheels).

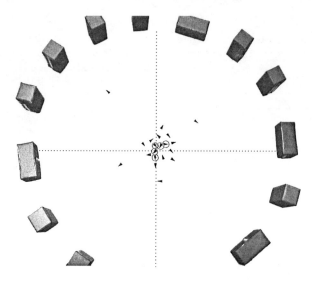

Figure 7.13: Performance based on mental transformation for detecting the center of the circle. Markers indicate the position of the robot's rotational axis and the direction the robot was facing. Markers surrounded by a circle represent trials in which the position was classified as center.

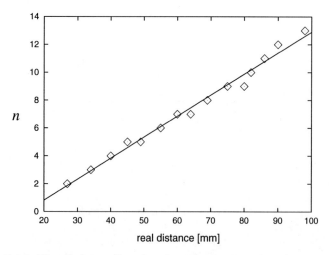

Figure 7.14: The number n of predicted steps toward an obstacle against the real distance to the obstacle. A line is fitted to the data.

7.4 Data outside the training domain

This section explains why a multi-layer perceptron that is trained to map data points within a sensory manifold, may map data points outside its training domain closer to the manifold (section 7.3.2, figure 7.11, left). This phenomenon depends on the structure of the training domain. It is not a general property of MLPs.

First, I show that all image vectors have about the same length, independent of the position of the robot. Second, I give a two-dimensional synthetic example having the same property. Third, I explain theoretically why in the example data points outside the training domain are mapped closer to the domain. Last, I show that the abstract RNN does not have this property in the example.

We estimate the length of an image vector **s** (the sensory representation). Although the world-to-camera mapping was non-linear, the image of the obstacle circle was still close to circular (figure 7.3). Its area was further almost independent of the robot's position. Thus, we assume that also on the camera image, the obstacles form a circle with fixed area. Within this region, the robot can stay at any point. To obtain the sensory representation, the circle is subdivided into ten sectors centered at the robot's position (figure 7.15).

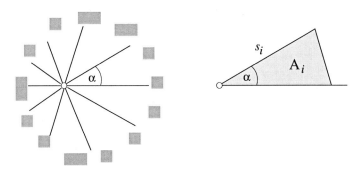

Figure 7.15: All sectors have the same angle α (left). A sector has a length s_i and an area A_i (right).

Let s_i be the length of each sector, and α be the angle of every sector (figure 7.15). If α is small enough then the area of a sector is well approximated by

$$A_i = \frac{1}{2}\alpha s_i^2 \ . \tag{7.2}$$

Therefore, the squared length of an image vector $\mathbf{s}$ equals

$$\|\mathbf{s}\|^2 = \sum_i s_i^2 = \sum_i \frac{2}{\alpha} A_i \approx \frac{2}{\alpha} A_\circ \ . \tag{7.3}$$

$A_\circ$ is the circle area enclosed by the obstacles. $A_\circ$ is independent of the position of the robot. Therefore, all training patterns lie on a 10-sphere (embedded in ten dimensions) with radius $\sqrt{2A_\circ/\alpha}$.

In the synthetic example discussed in the following, a circle is mapped onto a circle; that is, input and output are two-dimensional, and the training domain is a circle in the input and in the output space. The two circles would coincide if input and output coordinate system were put on top of each other. Each point $\mathbf{s}_i$ in the input circle has in the second circle a target point $\mathbf{g}_i$ that is rotated relative to $\mathbf{s}_i$ by 23° around the origin. 200 training points uniformly distributed around the circle were generated. An MLP learned the mapping from $\mathbf{s}_i$ to $\mathbf{g}_i$ for all $i = 1, \ldots, 200$. The MLP had a three layer structure composed of two input neurons, $h = 5$ hidden neurons, and two output neurons. In the hidden layer, the activation function was sigmoidal (tanh), and in the other layers, it was the identity function. Initially, the weights were drawn uniformly from the interval [-0.1; 0.1]. Using back-propagation in on-line mode, the network trained until convergence.

Figure 7.16 shows the result after training. Points outside the training domain (distance to the origin: 2.0) were mapped closer to the origin in the output space (distance around 1.5), and points inside the training domain (distance: 0.66) were mapped closer the unit circle (distance around 0.75).

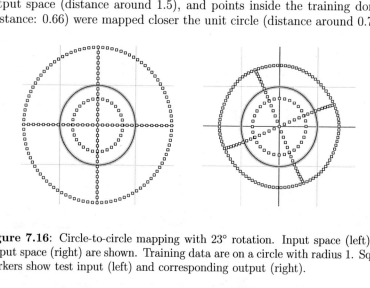

Figure 7.16: Circle-to-circle mapping with 23° rotation. Input space (left) and output space (right) are shown. Training data are on a circle with radius 1. Square markers show test input (left) and corresponding output (right).

In the following, this finding is studied theoretically. The MLP maps an input **s** to an output **o**,

$$o_i = \sum_{j=1}^{h} v_{ij} \tanh \left(\sum_{k=1}^{2} u_{jk} s_k \right) , \qquad (7.4)$$

with h hidden units and weight matrices **U** and **V**. If the activation function in the hidden layer would be the identity function then the output scales as the input. Multiplying the input by a scalar β gives

$$\mathbf{V} \mathbf{U} \beta \mathbf{s} = \beta \mathbf{V} \mathbf{U} \mathbf{s} . \qquad (7.5)$$

Here, outliers are not mapped closer to the circle. Thus, the observed contraction is caused by the sigmoidal activation function.

In the example with the two-dimensional circle, it was observed that in the trained network, the column vectors $\mathbf{u}_k$ of **U** were approximately orthogonal and had unit length; the same held for the row vectors[2] $\mathbf{v}_k$ of **V**. Thus, we assume that $\mathbf{u}_k^T \mathbf{u}_l = \delta_{kl}$ and $\mathbf{v}_k^T \mathbf{v}_l = \delta_{kl}$. With this assumption, it can be shown (appendix C.4) that points **s** outside the circle are mapped closer to the circle,

$$\|\mathbf{o}\| < \|\mathbf{s}\| . \qquad (7.6)$$

The theoretical explanation can be also extended to arbitrary dimensions with a hyper-sphere instead of a circle. In our robot task, however, the training patterns cannot cover all of the hyper-sphere because they are restricted to a two-dimensional manifold; in the synthetic example the whole circle is covered. This weakens the comparison.

The assumption $\mathbf{u}_k^T \mathbf{u}_l = \delta_{kl}$ further predicts that the contraction effect decreases with increasing number of neurons h in the hidden layer. The assumption infers that $\sum_{j=1}^{h} u_{jk}^2 = 1$. Thus, the expectation value of u_{jk}^2 equals $1/h$. The argument of tanh is $\sum_k u_{jk} s_k$. Here, the only random variables are $\{u_{jk}\}$, since the statement should hold for all **s**. Further, we assume that the expectation value of u_{jk} is zero. Then, for all inputs **s** with length β, the expectation value of the squared tanh-argument can be written as

---

[2]This is different for auto-associative networks with bottleneck hidden layer. For them, it can be shown that the column vectors of **V** tend to the principal components of the distribution $\{o_i\}$ (Diamantaras and Kung, 1996). Thus, for bottleneck networks, the *column* vectors are orthogonal.

$$\left\langle \left(\sum_{k=1}^{2} u_{jk} s_k \right)^2 \right\rangle = \sum_{k=1}^{2} \langle u_{jk}^2 \rangle s_k^2 = \frac{\beta^2}{h} \ . \tag{7.7}$$

The absolute mean value of the tanh-argument decreases with increasing h. Therefore, the tanh-function gets closer to the identity function, and the contraction effect weakens.

This finding was tested with the above experiment for different values of h. The result is shown in table 7.4. The values were averaged over three separately trained networks and on 360 trials each. The length of input vectors was set to 2.0. This experiment is in agreement with the above theoretical prediction.

hidden neurons	c
5	0.78
10	0.85
15	0.89
20	0.91
25	0.92

Table 7.4: Dependence of the mean contraction $c = \langle \|\mathbf{o}\| \rangle / \|\mathbf{s}\|$ on the number of hidden neurons.

Different from the MLP, the abstract RNN maintains the scale in the circle task (figure 7.17). The 200 pairs of circle points $(\mathbf{s}_i, \mathbf{g}_i)$ were approximated using a mixture of five units, each with two principal components (using for training MPPCA-ext). The centers of the ellipsoids turned out to be evenly distributed around the circle. Figure 7.17 shows that the distance to the origin is consistent between input and output pairs. As in (7.5), the local linear mappings do not change the length of input patterns.

7.5   Discussion

A chain of forward models could be applied to the planning of goal-directed movements and to mental transformation. The robot used the simulation of action sequences to perceive (to understand) its location within a circle of obstacles and to perceive the relative distance to obstacles. The forward model was acquired by random exploration. No teacher was necessary.

Tani (1996), Tani and Nolfi (1999), and Jirenhed et al. (2001) used also a chain of forward models for prediction. Different from our approach, they used Elman networks, which have a context layer (section 1.5.4). Such an

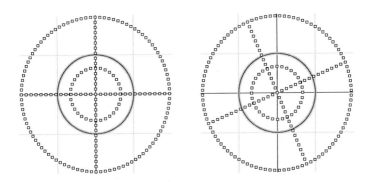

Figure 7.17: Circle-to-circle mapping with 23° rotation, using the abstract RNN. Input space (left) and output space (right) are shown. Training data are on a circle with radius 1. Square markers show test input (left) and corresponding output (right).

approach also allows goal-directed movements by optimizing the motor commands (Tani, 1996). However, the simulation of covert action is not possible because the robot needs to move to initialize its context layer (Tani, 1996). Therefore, in the presented study, context layers were omitted.

The forward model was trained either with a multi-layer perceptron or with an abstract recurrent neural network based on a mixture of local PCA. On the anticipation, the MLP was more accurate and 100-times faster than the abstract RNN. The MLP also had fewer free parameters: 355 free parameters for 12 input, 15 hidden, and ten output neurons against 6150 free parameters for a mixture model with 50 units and five principal components. Thus, the MLP was the favorable choice for the goal-directed movements and the mental transformation tasks.

On the standard training set, using a few principal components ($q = 5$), MPPCA-ext was better than NGPCA and NGPCA-constV. With the addition of two more components, however, MPPCA-ext got worse than the NGPCA variants. It was also worse than NGPCA-constV on a second training set ('change set') using seven or more principal components. An explanation for this apparent weakness for large q might be the following: a higher q leads to a smaller residual variance. Thus, the width of a local Gaussian probability density in the direction of the minor components is smaller. The stronger descent of this density in these directions leads to a likelihood (which is the product of the probabilities of all data points) that is more sensitive to the positions of single data points. Thus, MPPCA-ext is less robust since it maximizes this likelihood.

The introduction of the change set did not bring a noticeable difference to the maximal performance of the abstract RNN. However, it served to demonstrate that a higher noise-to-signal ratio for some of the components of a training pattern can be counterbalanced by adding more principal components in the mixture model (if using NGPCA-constV).

In the change set, the local variation extended into nine additional dimensions. This number possibly arises from two facts. First, the relative change of an image vector has ten components. Second, the length of an image vector is almost constant (as shown in section 7.4), which restricts the number of dimensions the variance can extend to.

NGPCA-constV was better on the change set than NGPCA, because it did not produce units that have only a few patterns assigned to them. This matches the observation in chapter 6.

The once trained abstract RNNs could also map in the inverse direction, that is, from two successive sensory states onto the wheel velocities. Here, however, the error was high (about 20% of the velocity range). The explanation is possibly the much larger number of input dimensions compared to output dimensions (20 to 2). Thus, as examined in section 4.6, the expected error is higher than for the forward direction (which maps from 12 to 10 dimensions).

Goal-directed motion planning requires a search in a high-dimensional motor space defined by a sequence of movements. Nothing is known about the structure of the optimization function defined over this space. The fact that Powell's method, which is a local minimization method, showed a similar performance like simulated annealing suggests that the presented task has few local minima that are not global. Whether other environments have similar properties is not known.

The square error in the goal-directed movement task was higher than the one observed in the prediction of random test series (compare table 7.3 with figure 7.9). The explanation is that the robot could not always execute successfully its given motor commands. The four wheels made the robot occasionally stick on the floor during slow turns. Such trials were omitted in the collection of test samples; however, they could not be avoided during goal-directed movements[3].

The low error for the anticipation (below 2.4 pixels squared, see figure 7.9) allowed a successful application to mental transformation. Here, a series of covert motor commands was simulated. The temporal characteristic of these motor commands was the same as for their overt execution; this matches human-behavioral findings (Jeannerod, 2001).

---

[3]An improvement would be a robot using only two driven wheels and caster wheels, which turns on a floor more easily.

The robot could detect the center of the circle of obstacles by simulating a turn around its rotational axis. The maximum distance of a location, classified as center, to the real center (10 cm) is low compared to the circle diameter (180 cm) and to the length of the robot (40 cm). The remaining inaccuracy might be attributed to prediction errors, and to deviations from perfect symmetry in the circle of obstacles.

The robot could also estimate the distance to an obstacle by simulating a straight-forward movement and predicting the first interval in which the activation in the frontal sector of the image representation was below a threshold. The number of this interval scaled with the real distance to the obstacle (figure 7.14). Since over-proportionally many examples were collected for straight-forward movements than for turns, the prediction in this task was more accurate than on average. A good performance was achieved for up to 13 prediction steps.

The judgment of relative distances based on sensorimotor integration relates to a psychological experiment by Sun et al. (2003). They showed that active movement improves visual-based estimation of path lengths. In this study, subjects rode an exercise bicycle, while wearing a virtual reality headset that presented a view along a corridor. Based on visual cues, the subjects had to estimate the length of the path traveled. The better the match between exercised movement and virtual movement, the more accurate was the estimation.

For the MLP and the abstract RNN, we observed that data points outside the sensory manifold were mapped back toward the sensory manifold. As shown in section 7.3.3, the restriction of predicted states to this manifold possibly explains why the prediction error increased slower than expected. Compared to the abstract RNN, the MLP was better at this backward mapping (figure 7.11 and section 7.4). This might explain why the MLP was more accurate.

Chapter 8

Conclusions

Unsupervised learning methods were developed and applied to sensorimotor models, which in turn were used to solve perceptual tasks. For each sensorimotor model the following three steps were pursued. First, data were collected and preprocessed. These data are distributed in a sensorimotor space, whose dimensions comprise all sensory variables and all motor variables. Second, this distribution was approximated by a simplified and generalizing representation. Third, upon this approximation, recall mechanisms were developed that could complete a partially given input pattern, and thus allowed the association of patterns. The advantage of the new learning methods over a multi-layer perceptron and a look-up table was demonstrated. Finally, it was shown how sensorimotor models can be used as a basis for the perception of object-shapes and space.

8.1 Data collection and preprocessing

Sensorimotor models were acquired in three setups: a kinematic arm model (section 4.5), a real robot arm equipped with a camera (chapter 6), and mobile robot also equipped with a camera (chapter 7). The raw data contained the following:

- For the kinematic arm model, the motor part are six joint angles, and the sensory part are the three corresponding coordinates of the end-effector and a collision variable.

- For the real robot arm, the motor part are the six joint angles of an arm posture suitable to grasp an object, and the sensory part is an image of the object.

- For the mobile robot, the motor part are the wheel velocities, and the sensory part are two successive images.

Training data were collected during random exploration; that is, the robot chose random motor commands and observed the sensory consequences of its actions. This exploration is the actual unsupervised part of the learning. Whether the following interpretation of this data is called unsupervised is more a matter of definition (see, for example, Meinicke (2000)).

Different from the kinematic arm model, the studies with the real robots revealed that it was necessary to preprocess the collected data. The dimensionality of the images was too high. The following three processing strategies proved to be useful:

- Keep positions (here, of an object or of the mobile robot) that are close together in Cartesian space also close together within the distribution of the preprocessed sensory data.

- Leave a residual redundancy in the preprocessed sensorimotor data. Population codes, as observed in nature, were a good example (chapter 6).

- Separate points in the final sensorimotor space that do not relate to each other, such as redundant arm posture for the same sensory input.

A processing that extracts lines, rectangles, or the like from an image was avoided. Including such more complex sensory representations may lead to the same conceptual problems as discussed for the symbolic approach (section 1.4.1). These representations depend on the designer's choice and may distract from the real difficulties of a behavioral task (Brooks, 1986b; Möller, 1999).

8.2 Approximation of the data distribution

Two strategies were pursued: either the distribution of sensorimotor data was approximated by a mixture of ellipsoids (chapter 3), or the distribution's mapping into a single higher-dimensional space was approximated by a hyperplane (chapter 5). The first was accomplished by a mixture of local principal component analyzers (PCA). Here, a single PCA operates on a region within the distribution. For each ellipsoid, the resulting principal components are the axes' directions, and the corresponding eigenvalues are the squared axes' lengths. To obtain the free parameters of the mixture model (the ellipsoids' centers, axes' directions and lengths) three new methods were presented:

- **NGPCA** is an extension of the vector quantizer Neural Gas (Martinetz et al., 1993) to local PCA (Möller and Hoffmann, 2004). For each presented data point, not only the centers are updated, but also the principal components. Herein, an error measure (the normalized Mahalanobis distance plus reconstruction error) regulates the competition between the units of the mixture (section 3.2.1).

- **NGPCA-constV** is a variant of NGPCA. Here, the error measure is replaced by one that removes the dependency on the volume of an ellipsoid (section 3.2.2).

- **MPPCA-ext** is an extension of the mixture of probabilistic PCA (Tipping and Bishop, 1999), which is a mixture of Gaussian probability functions that model the density of the data distribution (section 2.3.1). The algorithm was modified in three parts:

  First, Neural Gas was used to initialize the centers. Second, units with almost zero weight were moved to more dense regions within the distribution. And third, an on-line method for PCA was used, which allows the addition of noise to each presented data point (section 3.3). The last two parts made the algorithm usable for the sensorimotor distributions from the robot experiments. The sparseness of these distributions would otherwise lead to eigenvalues with zero value (section 6.2.5).

These algorithms were demonstrated to work on synthetic data and on the classification of hand-written digits (section 3.4). On classification tasks, however, mixture models are not the most suitable. Here, feed-forward networks and support-vector machines (Cortes and Vapnik, 1995) can do better (LeCun et al., 1998).

On most tasks, the NGPCA variants gave about the same performance than MPPCA-ext, though some differences were visible. The NGPCA variants were more sensitive than MPPCA-ext on the training parameters (section 3.5 and 6.3). Further, the dependence on these parameters is not understood.

On the other hand, the NGPCA variants could cope with arbitrarily many dimensions; MPPCA-ext fails on high-dimensional data (observed for 676 and 784 dimensions, see section 4.4.2 and 3.4). This problem arises from the Gaussian function, which vanishes for the large distances that the high-dimensional space provides (section 3.4.2). Thus, probably, this problem can be also found in other Gaussian mixture models (Tipping and Bishop, 1999; Albrecht et al., 2000; Meinicke and Ritter, 2001). These studies did not report tests on such high-dimensional data.

In the robot experiments, NGPCA-constV was observed to be better than NGPCA (section 6.3 and 7.3.2). This performance difference is possibly linked to the assignment of the data points among the units. For NGPCA-constV, this assignment was more balanced. In particular, more training patterns were assigned to the unit with the fewest patterns (section 6.3 and 7.3.2).

The mixture model parameters, the number of units and the number of principal components were defined before training. The first was set by trial and error. Using more units improved the performance until the point where the number of training patterns per unit was not sufficient for a robust training (section 4.5.2 and 5.3.2). The number of principal components was estimated from the local dimensionality of the distribution. This dimensionality was accessible experimentally by computing a PCA in the neighborhood of each data point (section 4.5.2, 6.2.5, and 7.2.5).

In the second strategy, which uses a hyper-plane to approximate the data distribution, the data were mapped into a higher-dimensional space, a so-called feature space. The algorithm 'kernel PCA' Schölkopf et al. (1998b) extracted the principal components of the data's mapping in this feature space (section 2.4). This algorithm does not require that the mapping is actually carried out; instead, all computation is done in the original space. The principal components in feature space spanned the hyper-plane that approximated the data.

8.3   Pattern association

Based on the two strategies for the approximation of the data distributions (section 8.2), two pattern-association methods were developed (chapter 4 and 5). In both methods, an input pattern was the offset from zero of a constrained subspace within the sensorimotor space. The span of this subspace was the output space.

In the first method, the constrained space intersected the mixture of ellipsoids. This computation could be carried out analytically. The resulting point yielded in its components the output pattern. In contrast to a gradient descent in a potential field build on top of the mixture of ellipsoids, the described approach does never end in a local minimum and has no additional parameters.

In the second method, a potential field was constructed. In feature space, the potential was the squared distance to the hyper-plane that approximated the data. A kernel function allowed to compute the potential in the original space. In this space, a gradient descent along the constraint gave the output.

Both methods have two advantages over feed-forward networks: First, input and output dimensions can be chosen *after* training. In particular, for sensorimotor models, the association works in both forward and inverse direction. Second, the association does not fail if the training set contains redundant output patterns for a single input. The first advantage was demonstrated on the completion of images (section 4.4.1), on the kinematic arm model (section 4.5), and by using the sensorimotor model for the mobile robot as an inverse model (section 7.3.2). The second advantage was demonstrated on the kinematic arm model (section 4.5) and on the robot arm (chapter 6). The robot arm could recall a suitable arm posture to grasp an object seen in the camera, despite the fact that redundant arm postures existed.

These two advantages were also demonstrated in recurrent neural networks (Steinkühler and Cruse, 1998). Therefore, we called the first method abstract recurrent neural network. The argument also holds for the second method. However, to distinguish the two clearly, just one was called abstract RNN.

The recall with the mixture model was more accurate and faster than with kernel PCA (section 5.3.2 and 6.3). Thus, the emphasis was on the mixture model. Nevertheless, kernel PCA demonstrated that with increasing dimensionality a data distribution can be better described with a linear model. This matches two further observations. First, a single PCA did well on the completion of images, which had more dimensions than the sensorimotor data in the other tasks (section 4.4). Second, in the robot-arm experiment, the mixture of local PCA did better on a higher-dimensional training set, which comprised population coded variables (chapter 6).

8.4 Results compared to other methods

The abstract RNN was compared to a multi-layer perceptron (MLP) and to a look-up table. This section further points out differences to the pattern-association based on self-organizing maps (SOM) (Ritter et al., 1990) and to the pattern-association based on parametrized self-organizing maps (PSOM) (Ritter, 1993).

Section 8.3 mentioned some tasks to which the abstract RNN can be applied but the MLP cannot. In tasks that only require to learn a function from input to output (many-to-one or one-to-one), the results are less distinct. In the forward direction of the kinematic arm model, the abstract RNN did better than the MLP (section 4.5); however, in the mobile-robot experiment, the MLP did better on the prediction of the sensory input (section 7.3.2).

We observed that the performance of the abstract RNN deteriorated the more input against output dimensions were chosen (section 4.5.2 and 4.6). This suggests that for tasks in which the input dimensions outnumber the output dimensions (for example, by 20 to 2), the MLP should be preferred.

This dependence on the number of input dimensions also holds for a look-up table that picks the best fit among all training patterns (section 4.6). In contrast to a look-up table, however, the abstract RNN could interpolate between patterns and thus resulted in more accurate associations (section

4.4.2 and 6.3). Moreover, with the addition of noise to the training patterns, the performance of the abstract RNN did not deteriorate as much as in the look-up-table case (section 6.3).

Compared to the algorithms SOM and PSOM (see section 1.5.5 and 1.5.6), the abstract RNN has the following advantages:

- SOM: The abstract RNN can cope with distributions of higher local dimensionality. A single ellipsoid can cover a region for which many SOM-grid points would be needed (section 3.1).

- SOM: The abstract RNN could cope with redundancy in the target values (section 4.5 and chapter 6).

- PSOM: The abstract RNN could be applied to data distributions with unknown topology (for example, images, section 4.4).

- PSOM: The abstract RNN could cope with distributions that are discontinuous (section 4.5).

- SOM and PSOM: The abstract RNN could cope with additional noise dimensions (section 4.5.2).

8.5   Perception

Based on sensorimotor models, the present work showed how visual perception might emerge:

- The location and orientation of an object within the reach of an arm could be perceived by simulating an arm posture suitable to grasp the object. This simulation was demonstrated with the robot arm (chapter 6). The abstract RNN associated an arm posture given an image representation of the object. The arm posture represented the real location and orientation accurately (mean distance between gripper tip and object: about 7 mm, mean difference in orientation: about 4°).

- The geometry of the surrounding world, the real distance to obstacles, could be perceived by 'mentally' simulating a movement toward the obstacles. This simulation was carried out in the mobile robot (chapter 7). The robot predicted the number of 2 sec intervals required to reach an obstacle in front.

- Symmetry within the world could also be perceived by simulating a movement. This kind of perception was demonstrated on the example of a circle (chapter 7). A simulated turn in the center of the circle predicts an invariant visual input, and this invariance can be observed only at the center. This way, humans might detect symmetry, despite having a distorted sensory representation in the visual cortex.

These experiments show that perception of space and shape can be explained by the sensorimotor approach. Instead of using a pure sensory representation, all is reduced to the simulation of motor commands and their sensory consequences.

In the mobile-robot study, depth perception was based on computing the time-to-contact; in the robot-arm study, depth perception was based on associating an arm posture. This difference implies that for unlike tasks different spatial representations exist, for example, a far field for locomotion and a near field for grasping (Mallot et al., 1992).

8.6 Future direction

The present work can be extended in several directions:

- To remove the sensitivity of NGPCA and NGPCA-constV on the parameters, an automatic adjustment during the training would be helpful. A further helpful extension would be a growing mixture model that adjusts the number of units m and principal components q to the data distribution. For the Neural Gas vector quantizer, Fritzke (1995) developed a model that adjusts m. Meinicke and Ritter (2001) extended MPPCA to adjust q.

- Moreover, for NGPCA, different error measures or different ranking functions might avoid 'dead units' and thin ellipsoids that protrude out of a distribution (see section 3.3.2, figure 3.8 and the discussion in section 3.5).

- The recall in the abstract RNN has discontinuities (for more than one unit). An interpolation between neighboring units might lead to better results.

- So far, the robot arm did only *grasp* objects. A possible extension is to include object manipulation. By mentally simulating such a manipulation, the robot could recognize the object, as in the following example. Two objects need to be recognized: a cylinder and a brick (as in chapter 6). Both lie on the table. If the robot pushes the cylinder, it will roll; if the robot pushes the brick, it will move only a short distance. Once trained, the robot sees an object with its camera. Using simulation, the robot can predict what would happen to the object if pushed. Based on the outcome, the robot can decide if it was a cylinder or a brick. If this experiment also works for different illuminations and different object orientations, it could show that the sensorimotor approach can explain object constancy.

- The mobile-robot experiment may be extended to the perception of dead-ends, as suggested by Möller (1999). Standing in front of a potential dead-end, the robot simulates the outcome of an obstacle-avoidance algorithm. If the robot predicts that it will get stuck, it can conclude that it faces a dead-end. With the same mechanism, dead-ends of different shape and seen from different perspectives could be perceived (object constancy).

- The abstract RNN could be helpful for other applications. It could be applied to any pattern-association with locally continuous mappings between patterns.

Appendix A

Statistical tools

A.1 Bayes' theorem

The probability $p(\mathbf{x}, j)$ of observing both $\mathbf{x}$ and j can be written in two ways,

$$p(\mathbf{x}, j) = p(\mathbf{x}|j)P(j) = P(j|\mathbf{x})p(\mathbf{x}) \ . \tag{A.1}$$

$p(\mathbf{x})$ is the probability of $\mathbf{x}$ (independent of j), $P(j)$ is the probability of j (independent of $\mathbf{x}$), $p(\mathbf{x}|j)$ is the probability of $\mathbf{x}$ under the condition that j is given, and $P(j|\mathbf{x})$ is the probability of j under the condition that $\mathbf{x}$ is given. Reorganizing (A.1) about $P(j|\mathbf{x})$ gives

$$P(j|\mathbf{x}) = \frac{p(\mathbf{x}|j)P(j)}{p(\mathbf{x})} \ . \tag{A.2}$$

This is Bayes' theorem.

A.2 Maximum likelihood

The maximum likelihood principle is illustrated in an example with a one-dimensional data distribution $\{x_i\}$, $i = 1, ..., n$. We assume that the data originate from a Gaussian distribution $p(x)$ with parameters σ and μ,

$$p(x) = \frac{1}{\sqrt{2\pi}\sigma} \exp\left(-\frac{(x - \mu)^2}{2\sigma^2}\right) \ . \tag{A.3}$$

According to the maximum likelihood principle, we will choose the unknown parameters such that the given data are most likely under the obtained distribution. The probability L of the given data set is

$$L(\sigma, \mu) = \prod_{i=1}^{n} p(x_i) = \left(\frac{1}{\sqrt{2\pi}\sigma}\right)^n \exp\left(-\frac{\sum_{i=1}^{n}(x_i - \mu)^2}{2\sigma^2}\right) \ . \tag{A.4}$$

We want to find $\hat{\sigma}$ and $\hat{\mu}$ that maximize L. Maximizing L is equivalent to maximizing $\log L$, which is also called the log-likelihood $\mathcal{L}$,

$$\mathcal{L}(\sigma, \mu) = \log L(\sigma, \mu) = -n \log \sigma - \frac{\sum_i (x_i - \mu)^2}{2\sigma^2} + \text{const} \ . \tag{A.5}$$

To find the maximum we compute the derivatives of the log-likelihood $\mathcal{L}$ and set them to zero:

$$\frac{\partial \mathcal{L}}{\partial \sigma} = -\frac{n}{\sigma} + \frac{\sum_i (x_i - \mu)^2}{\sigma^3} \overset{!}{=} 0 \ , \tag{A.6}$$

$$\frac{\partial \mathcal{L}}{\partial \mu} = \frac{\sum_i (x_i - \mu)}{\sigma^2} \overset{!}{=} 0 \ . \tag{A.7}$$

Thus, we obtain the values of the parameters $\hat{\sigma}$ and $\hat{\mu}$:

$$\hat{\sigma}^2 = \frac{\sum_i (x_i - \hat{\mu})^2}{n} \ , \tag{A.8}$$

$$\hat{\mu} = \frac{\sum_i x_i}{n} \ . \tag{A.9}$$

The resulting $\hat{\sigma}^2$ is the variance of the distribution and $\hat{\mu}$ is its center. The extremum of $\mathcal{L}$ is indeed a local maximum, as can be seen by computing the Hesse matrix of $\mathcal{L}$ and evaluating it at the extreme point $(\hat{\sigma}, \hat{\mu})$:

$$H_{\mathcal{L}} = \begin{vmatrix} \frac{\partial^2 \mathcal{L}}{\partial \sigma^2} & \frac{\partial^2 \mathcal{L}}{\partial \sigma \partial \mu} \\ \\ \frac{\partial^2 \mathcal{L}}{\partial \mu \partial \sigma} & \frac{\partial^2 \mathcal{L}}{\partial \mu^2} \end{vmatrix} \ , \tag{A.10}$$

$$\frac{\partial^2 \mathcal{L}}{\partial \sigma^2} \Big|_{\sigma = \hat{\sigma}, \mu = \hat{\mu}} = \frac{n}{\hat{\sigma}^2} - \frac{3 \sum_i (x_i - \hat{\mu})^2}{\hat{\sigma}^4} = \frac{n}{\hat{\sigma}^2} - \frac{3n\hat{\sigma}^2}{\hat{\sigma}^4} = -\frac{2n}{\hat{\sigma}^2} \ , \tag{A.11}$$

$$\frac{\partial^2 \mathcal{L}}{\partial \sigma \partial \mu} \Big|_{\sigma = \hat{\sigma}, \mu = \hat{\mu}} = \frac{\partial^2 \mathcal{L}}{\partial \mu \partial \sigma} \Big|_{\sigma = \hat{\sigma}, \mu = \hat{\mu}} = -\frac{2 \sum_i (x_i - \hat{\mu})}{\hat{\sigma}^3} = 0 \ ,$$

$$\frac{\partial^2 \mathcal{L}}{\partial \mu^2} \Big|_{\sigma = \hat{\sigma}, \mu = \hat{\mu}} = -\frac{n}{\hat{\sigma}^2} \ .$$

It follows that the Hesse matrix at the extremum is negative definite,

$$H_{\mathcal{L}}|_{\sigma = \hat{\sigma}, \mu = \hat{\mu}} = \begin{vmatrix} -\frac{2n}{\hat{\sigma}^2} & 0 \\ \\ 0 & -\frac{n}{\hat{\sigma}^2} \end{vmatrix} \ . \tag{A.12}$$

Therefore, the extremum is a local maximum. Moreover, it is also a global maximum. First, for finite parameters, no other extrema exist because $\mathcal{L}$ is a smooth function. Second, $\mathcal{L}$ is positive for finite parameters, but approaches zero for infinite values. Thus, any maximum must be in the finite range.

A.3 Iterative mean

The mean value of a distribution $\{x_i\}$ can also be computed iteratively if the values x_i are drawn one-by-one. Let $\langle x \rangle_t$ be the average over the first t data points. We observe that

$$
\begin{aligned}
\langle x \rangle_t &= \frac{1}{t} \sum_{i=1}^{t} x_i \\
&= \frac{1}{t} \sum_{i=1}^{t-1} x_i + \frac{1}{t} x_t \\
&= \frac{t-1}{t} \frac{1}{t-1} \sum_{i=1}^{t-1} x_i + \frac{1}{t} x_t \\
&= \frac{t-1}{t} \langle x \rangle_{t-1} + \frac{1}{t} x_t \; .
\end{aligned}
\tag{A.13}
$$

Thus, the update rule for the temporary mean $c(t+1) = \langle x \rangle_t$ upon presentation of a value x is

$$
c(t+1) = c(t) + \frac{1}{t+1} (x - c(t)) \; .
\tag{A.14}
$$

This rule is the same as for the center update in vector quantization with a learning rate that decays as $1/t$.

Appendix B

Algorithms

B.1 Power method with deflation

The power method is a common method to extract the eigenvector with the largest eigenvalue (Diamantaras and Kung, 1996). Starting with a random vector $\mathbf{a}$, the principal eigenvector of a matrix $\mathbf{K}$ is computed by iterating:

$$\frac{\mathbf{Ka}}{\|\max(\mathbf{Ka})\|} \rightarrow \mathbf{a} \ . \tag{B.1}$$

$\max(\mathbf{Ka})$ is the component of the vector $\mathbf{Ka}$ with the largest absolute value (some variants of the power method use $\|\mathbf{a}\|$ instead). This iteration converges to the largest eigenvector with the eigenvalue $\lambda' = \|\max(\mathbf{Ka})\|$. Further eigenvectors are obtained using deflation. After the eigenvector $\mathbf{a}_i$ (number i, ordered by the size of the corresponding eigenvalue) is computed, a new matrix $\mathbf{K}_{i+1}$ is obtained from the previous one $\mathbf{K}_i$ by iterating

$$\mathbf{K}_{i+1} = \mathbf{K}_i - \lambda'_i \frac{\mathbf{a}_i \mathbf{a}_i^T}{\mathbf{a}_i^T \mathbf{a}_i} \ , \tag{B.2}$$

where λ'_i is the eigenvalue corresponding to $\mathbf{a}_i$.

B.2 Kernel PCA speed-up

The computational load for the projection onto a principal component is high, n evaluations of $k(\mathbf{z}, \mathbf{x}_i)$. In the context of support vector machines, Burges (1996) introduced a speed-up usable for the extraction of the principal components (Schölkopf et al. (1998b) suggested that this could be also used for kernel PCA). The idea is to approximate each vector $\mathbf{w} = \sum_{i=1}^{n} \alpha_i \boldsymbol{\varphi}(\mathbf{x}_i)$ by another vector $\mathbf{w}'$ using only a small set of vectors $\mathbf{y}_i$ from the original space, instead of the whole set $\{\mathbf{x}_i\}$,

$$\mathbf{w}' = \sum_{i=1}^{m} \beta_i \boldsymbol{\varphi}(\mathbf{y}_i) \ . \tag{B.3}$$

m is set a priori to a value much smaller than n. The set $\{(\mathbf{y}_i, \beta_i) \,|\, i = 1, \ldots, m\}$ is called reduced set (Burges, 1996).

Here, instead of minimizing $||\mathbf{w} - \mathbf{w}'||^2$ to determine the reduced set, we use a method introduced by Schölkopf et al. (1998a). It is computationally expensive to optimize over the whole reduced set simultaneously; thus instead, an iterative method extracts the $\mathbf{y}_i$ one by one. Moreover, the optimization over $\mathbf{y}_i$ and β_i is split.

First, starting with $\mathbf{y}_1$, we minimize the distance between $\mathbf{w}$ and its projection onto the span of $\boldsymbol{\varphi}(\mathbf{y}_1)$,

$$\min_{\mathbf{y}_1} \left(\left\| \frac{\mathbf{w}^T \boldsymbol{\varphi}(\mathbf{y}_1)}{\boldsymbol{\varphi}(\mathbf{y}_1)^T \boldsymbol{\varphi}(\mathbf{y}_1)} \boldsymbol{\varphi}(\mathbf{y}_1) - \mathbf{w} \right\|^2 \right) \ . \tag{B.4}$$

Minimizing this distance is equivalent to maximizing

$$\frac{\left(\mathbf{w}^T \boldsymbol{\varphi}(\mathbf{y}_1) \right)^2}{\boldsymbol{\varphi}(\mathbf{y}_1)^T \boldsymbol{\varphi}(\mathbf{y}_1)} = \frac{\left(\sum_{i=1}^{n} \alpha_i k(\mathbf{x}_i, \mathbf{y}_1) \right)^2}{k(\mathbf{y}_1, \mathbf{y}_1)} \ . \tag{B.5}$$

This optimization problem is much less demanding than the before mentioned, the dimensionality is the one of the pattern space. The denominator is constant for radial basis function kernels. Here, only the numerator needs to be maximized.

After $\mathbf{y}_1$ is determined, the optimal β_1 is computed. Generally, if the values $\mathbf{y}_i$ are known, the corresponding optimal β_i can be obtained analytically by setting the derivatives $\frac{\partial}{\partial \beta_i} ||\mathbf{w} - \mathbf{w}'||^2$ zero (Schölkopf et al., 1998a). The result is

$$\boldsymbol{\beta} = (\mathbf{K}^y)^{-1} \mathbf{K}^{yx} \boldsymbol{\alpha} \ . \tag{B.6}$$

K^y is the matrix $k(\mathbf{y}_i, \mathbf{y}_j)$, and K^{yx} the matrix $k(\mathbf{y}_i, \mathbf{x}_j)$.

$\beta_1 \boldsymbol{\varphi}(\mathbf{y}_1)$ alone is not enough to replace $\mathbf{w}$. Therefore, the second point $\mathbf{y}_2$ is chosen such that the remaining vector $\mathbf{w} - \beta_1 \boldsymbol{\varphi}(\mathbf{y}_1)$ is approximated by $\beta_2 \boldsymbol{\varphi}(\mathbf{y}_2)$. This leads to an iterative scheme, with $\mathbf{w}_{t+1} = \mathbf{w}_t - \beta_t \boldsymbol{\varphi}(\mathbf{y}_t)$, starting with $\mathbf{w}_1 = \mathbf{w}$. At each step, $\mathbf{w}_t$ is approximated by $\beta_t \boldsymbol{\varphi}(\mathbf{y}_t)$. That is, $\mathbf{y}_t$ is obtained by maximizing (B.5), and then, $\{\beta_i \,|\, i = 1, \ldots, t\}$ are calculated using (B.6). Every iteration step, every addition of a set $(\mathbf{y}_t, \beta_t)$, reduces the distance to the vector $\mathbf{w}$. In this way, the complete reduced set can be obtained.

In kernel PCA, more than one vector needs to be approximated. To do this, the above method can be generalized (Schölkopf et al., 1998a). Instead of (B.4), the sum of the square projection distances is minimized,

$$\min_{\mathbf{y}_t} \left(\sum_{l=0}^{q} \left\| \frac{\mathbf{w}^{l^T} \varphi(\mathbf{y}_t)}{\varphi(\mathbf{y}_t)^T \varphi(\mathbf{y}_t)} \varphi(\mathbf{y}_t) - \mathbf{w}^l \right\|^2 \right) . \tag{B.7}$$

Here, $\mathbf{w}^0$ is the center vector $\frac{1}{n} \sum_{i=1}^{n} \varphi(\mathbf{x}_i)$; and $\mathbf{w}^l$, with $l = 1, \ldots, q$, are the q eigenvectors $\sum_{i=1}^{n} \alpha_i^l \varphi(\mathbf{x}_i)$. The iteration is the same as above, $\mathbf{w}_{t+1}^l = \mathbf{w}_t^l - \beta_t^l \varphi(\mathbf{y}_t)$. The β_i^l are computed for each vector separately, $\boldsymbol{\beta}^l = (\mathbf{K}^y)^{-1} \mathbf{K}^{yx} \boldsymbol{\alpha}^l$. However, each approximated vector is based on the same set $\{\mathbf{y}_i\}$.

The result of this reduced set method is that all vectors that are expressed as a sum over n kernel functions, can be obtained as a sum over only m kernel functions. Thus, the speed gain is n/m.

B.3 Quality measure for a potential field

In this section a method is introduced that determines the quality of the match between a potential field and a data distribution $\{\mathbf{x}_i\}$. The overlap is computed between the data distribution and a region of same volume enclosed by an iso-potential curve (figure B.1). The method relies on the data points being uniformly distributed over a closed region $\mathcal{G}$ with volume A (as it is the case for the ring-line-square and vortex distributions).

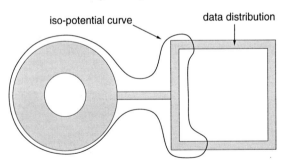

Figure B.1: Illustration of an iso-potential curve surrounding a region of same volume as the data distribution.

Let B_c be the volume of the closed region defined by $\{\mathbf{x} \mid p(\mathbf{x}) \le c\}$, which is the set of points surrounded by an iso-potential curve with value c. The volume B_c was calculated using Monte-Carlo integration.

The computation of the quality measure has two steps. First, choose c, such that $B_c = A$. Second, count the number of data points $\mathbf{x}_i$ fulfilling $p(\mathbf{x}_i) \leq c$. The quality measure is the percentage of this number on the total number of data points.

Appendix C

Proofs

C.1 Probabilistic PCA and error measures

In probabilistic principal component analysis, the observed d-dimensional data $\{x_i\}$ are assumed to origin from a probability density $p(x)$. This density can be written as

$$p(x) = (2\pi)^{-d/2}(\det B)^{-1/2} \exp\left(-\frac{1}{2}(x-c)^T B^{-1}(x-c)\right) , \qquad (C.1)$$

with $B = \sigma^2 I_d + UU^T$ (Tipping and Bishop, 1997). I_d is the d-dimensional identity matrix, and σ^2 is the noise variance. The $d \times q$ matrix U is obtained by maximizing the likelihood of the data $\{x_i\}$ given the probability $p(x)$. Tipping and Bishop (1999) showed that the result is

$$U = W(\Lambda - \sigma^2 I_q)^{1/2} R . \qquad (C.2)$$

The columns of the $d \times q$ matrix W are the q principal eigenvectors of the covariance matrix of $\{x_i\}$. The q largest eigenvalues λ_j of the covariance matrix are the entries of the diagonal matrix Λ. R is an arbitrary $q \times q$ rotational matrix.

In the following, it is shown that the double negative logarithm of (C.1) equals the normalized Mahalanobis distance plus reconstruction error (section 3.2.1) plus a constant. Using (C.2) to rewrite the expression for B gives

$$B = \sigma^2 I_d + W(\Lambda - \sigma^2 I_q)W^T = W\Lambda W^T + \sigma^2(I_d - WW^T) . \qquad (C.3)$$

By showing that $BB^{-1} = I$ and $B^{-1}B = I$, we can verify that the inverse of B is

$$B^{-1} = W\Lambda^{-1}W^T + \frac{1}{\sigma^2}(I_d - WW^T) . \qquad (C.4)$$

The eigenvalues of $\mathbf{B}$ are $\lambda_1, ..., \lambda_q$ and σ^2. The latter occurs $(d-q)$-times. Thus, the determinant of $\mathbf{B}$ is

$$\det \mathbf{B} = \left(\sigma^2\right)^{d-q} \prod_{j=1}^{q} \lambda_j \; . \tag{C.5}$$

Finally, we evaluate the logarithm of $p(\mathbf{x})$ using (C.1), (C.4), and (C.5):

$$\ln p(\mathbf{x}) = -\frac{d}{2}\ln(2\pi) - \frac{1}{2}E(\mathbf{x} - \mathbf{c}) \tag{C.6}$$

with

$$E(\boldsymbol{\xi}) = \boldsymbol{\xi}^T \mathbf{W}\boldsymbol{\Lambda}^{-1}\mathbf{W}^T\boldsymbol{\xi} + \frac{1}{\sigma^2}(\boldsymbol{\xi}^T\boldsymbol{\xi} - \boldsymbol{\xi}^T\mathbf{W}\mathbf{W}^T\boldsymbol{\xi}) + \sum_{j}\ln\lambda_j + (d-q)\ln\sigma^2 , \tag{C.7}$$

and $\boldsymbol{\xi} = \mathbf{x} - \mathbf{c}$. E is a normalized Mahalanobis distance plus reconstruction error.

C.2 The eigenvalue equation in kernel PCA

The equivalence of the equations

$$n\lambda\mathbf{K}\boldsymbol{\alpha} = \mathbf{K}\mathbf{K}\boldsymbol{\alpha} \tag{C.8}$$

and

$$n\lambda\,\boldsymbol{\alpha} = \mathbf{K}\boldsymbol{\alpha} \tag{C.9}$$

is shown.

Equation (C.8) follows immediately from (C.9). To prove the opposite direction, we assume that a vector $\boldsymbol{\beta}$ exists that is not an eigenvector of $\mathbf{K}$, while $\mathbf{K}\boldsymbol{\beta}$ is an eigenvector of $\mathbf{K}$. This assumption infers that (C.8) is fulfilled and (C.9) is not. Thus, we need to show that the assumption leads to a contradiction.

We only consider the case that $\boldsymbol{\beta}$ is orthogonal to the subspace ker $\mathbf{K}$ (the space of vectors $\boldsymbol{\alpha}$ fulfilling $\mathbf{K}\boldsymbol{\alpha} = 0$) because the elements of ker $\mathbf{K}$—if they exist—solve already both (C.8) and (C.9). Since $\mathbf{K}$ is symmetric, $\boldsymbol{\beta}$ can be written as a linear combination of the pairwise orthogonal eigenvectors $\boldsymbol{\alpha}^l$ of $\mathbf{K}$, $\boldsymbol{\beta} = \sum_l u_l \boldsymbol{\alpha}^l$. At least, two u_l must differ from zero because $\boldsymbol{\beta}$ itself is not an eigenvector. It follows that $\mathbf{K}\boldsymbol{\beta} = \sum_l u_l\lambda_l'\boldsymbol{\alpha}^l$ with λ_l' being the eigenvalues corresponding to $\boldsymbol{\alpha}^l$. All eigenvalues are non-zero because $\boldsymbol{\beta}$ is orthogonal to ker $\mathbf{K}$. Thus, $\mathbf{K}\boldsymbol{\beta}$ can be also not an eigenvector of $\mathbf{K}$. This contradicts our first assumption. Therefore, (C.9) follows from (C.8).

C.3 Estimate of error accumulation

This section shows that the expectation value of the square error of the anticipated sensory input increases only linearly with the number of anticipation steps (Hoffmann and Möller, 2004). Let $\mathbf{e}$ be the error of the feed-forward output after a single step. $\mathbf{e}$ is a vector with one component for each output component. We assume that the probability distribution of this error is independent of the input to the network. Thus, all errors are independent of each other. In addition, we assume that the error for each output component has zero mean and the same standard deviation σ.

On this basis, we compute the expectation value of the square error. The total error of the chain output is the sum of the errors of the outputs of each link. To illustrate this, think of each correct transformation at one link as a line in a d-dimensional space, with d equal to the number of output components (figure C.1).

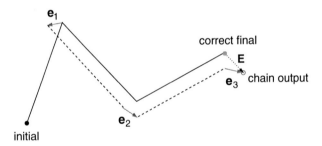

Figure C.1: Error accumulation in a feed-forward chain. Each solid black line is the correct transformation for one link. A dashed line is the correct transformation for a slightly different starting point.

A line connects an input point with an output point (of the transformation). The error at link i can be drawn as an arrow $\mathbf{e}_i$ at the end of a line (output point). This will result in a different starting point for the next line. If the error is small[1] and the transformation function sufficiently smooth, we can approximate that the displacement of the starting point does not change the direction and length of the next line, which is the correct transformation at the new starting point. Thus, the displacement $\mathbf{E}$ of the final point is the sum of the vectorial errors of each stage. Therefore, given l links, the total

---

[1]For the MLP, the square error stayed below 2.4 pixels squared, which is low compared to the range of values observed in figure 7.4: the square difference between the largest and the smallest value is about 500 pixels squared.

error E can be written as

$$E = \left\| \sum_{i=1}^{l} \mathbf{e}_i \right\| . \tag{C.10}$$

We compute the expectation value of E^2,

$$\langle E^2 \rangle = \left\langle \left\| \sum_{i=1}^{l} \mathbf{e}_i \right\|^2 \right\rangle . \tag{C.11}$$

Doing the square operation on the sum gives

$$\langle E^2 \rangle = \left\langle \sum_i \mathbf{e}_i^T \mathbf{e}_i + \sum_{i,j \neq i} \mathbf{e}_i^T \mathbf{e}_j \right\rangle , \tag{C.12}$$

and using the linear property of the expectation value results in

$$\begin{aligned} \langle E^2 \rangle &= \sum_i \langle \mathbf{e}_i^T \mathbf{e}_i \rangle + \sum_{i,j \neq i} \langle \mathbf{e}_i^T \mathbf{e}_j \rangle \\ &= \sum_i \langle \mathbf{e}_i^T \mathbf{e}_i \rangle . \end{aligned} \tag{C.13}$$

The last term vanishes because $\mathbf{e}_i$ and $\mathbf{e}_j$ are independent random variables, for $i \neq j$, and each variable has zero mean. The remainder is a sum over the variances for each link and dimension. Therefore,

$$\langle E^2 \rangle = l \, d \, \sigma^2 . \tag{C.14}$$

Thus, the expectation value of the square error increases only linearly with the chain length.

C.4   Contraction of input vectors

This section shows that a multi-layer perceptron maps data points outside its training domain closer to its domain if the perceptron is trained to map data distributed in a circle onto the same circle (see section 7.4). Let $\beta \mathbf{s}$ be the input to the trained network. Here, $\mathbf{s}$ has unit length and β is a scalar.

We study the effect of β on the network output $\mathbf{o}$. Let $\mathbf{U}$ be a $h \times 2$ matrix containing the weights between the input and the hidden layer, and $\mathbf{V}$ be a $2 \times h$ matrix with the weights between the hidden and the output layer. Further, let $\mathbf{u}_k$ be a column vector of $\mathbf{U}$, and $\mathbf{v}_k$ be a row vector of $\mathbf{V}$. We assume that all threshold values equal zero, and that the weights fulfill: $\mathbf{u}_k^T \mathbf{u}_l = \delta_{kl}$ and $\mathbf{v}_k^T \mathbf{v}_l = \delta_{kl}$.

We first look at the case $\beta = 1$. The network output is

$$o_i(1) = \sum_{j=1}^{h} v_{ij} \tanh \left(\sum_{k=1}^{2} u_{jk} s_k \right) \ . \tag{C.15}$$

As a result of the network training, $\mathbf{o}(1)$ has unit length. Let $\mathbf{y} = \mathbf{Us}$ be the argument of the tanh-function. From the assumptions follows that $\mathbf{y}$ has unit length,

$$||\mathbf{y}||^2 = \left\| \sum_{k=1}^{2} s_k \mathbf{u}_k \right\|^2 = \sum_{k=1}^{2} s_k^2 = 1 \ . \tag{C.16}$$

Thus, the states $\mathbf{y}$ lie on a circle with radius one and spanned by $\{\mathbf{u}_k\}$ in a h-dimensional space (figure C.2).

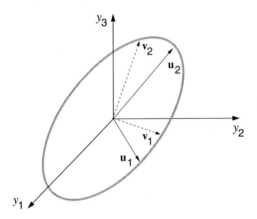

Figure C.2: Image of the training patterns (gray ellipse) in the space of the hidden neurons (here, $h = 3$). The circle lies on a plane spanned by $\{\mathbf{u}_k\}$. The vectors $\{\mathbf{v}_k\}$ lie in the same plane.

Let $\tilde{\mathbf{y}}$ be the vector with components $\tanh(y_j)$. A larger number h of hidden units leads to smaller components of $\mathbf{y}$ (section 7.4: y_j equals on average $1/h$). Therefore, we approximate $\tanh(y_j) \approx y_j$. It follows that also $\tilde{\mathbf{y}}$ lies on the circle in the span of $\{\mathbf{u}_k\}$.

Next, we look at the effect of the weight matrix $\mathbf{V}$. After training, all $\mathbf{x}$ (which have unit length) are mapped (C.15) onto a circle with radius one. Thus, $\mathbf{V}$ needs to project the circle in the span of $\{\mathbf{u}_k\}$ onto the unit circle in the two-dimensional output space. This is only achieved if both row vectors

$\mathbf{v}_1$ and $\mathbf{v}_2$ lie in the span of $\{\mathbf{u}_k\}$ (otherwise, the projection would be an ellipse). It follows that $\tilde{\mathbf{y}}$ is also in the span of $\{\mathbf{v}_k\}$, and any vector $\tilde{\mathbf{y}}$ in the span of $\{\mathbf{v}_k\}$ can be written as $\tilde{\mathbf{y}} = \sum_k (\tilde{\mathbf{y}}^T \mathbf{v}_k) \mathbf{v}_k$.

Next, we look at the case $\beta > 1$. Let $\tilde{\mathbf{y}}(\beta)$ be the vector with components $\tanh(\beta y_j)$. Here, the above tanh-approximation is generally not valid, and $\tilde{\mathbf{y}}(\beta)$ might protrude out of the plane spanned by $\{\mathbf{v}_k\}$. Thus, we need to write $\tilde{\mathbf{y}}(\beta) = \sum_k (\tilde{\mathbf{y}}(\beta)^T \mathbf{v}_k) \mathbf{v}_k + \mathbf{b}$, with $\mathbf{b}$ orthogonal to $\{\mathbf{v}_k\}$. The squares of this equation fulfill $||\tilde{\mathbf{y}}(\beta)||^2 = \sum_k ||\tilde{\mathbf{y}}(\beta)^T \mathbf{v}_k||^2 + ||\mathbf{b}||^2$, from which follows:

$$\sum_k ||\tilde{\mathbf{y}}(\beta)^T \mathbf{v}_k||^2 \leq ||\tilde{\mathbf{y}}(\beta)||^2 \ . \tag{C.17}$$

Therefore, for $\beta > 1$, the squared length of the output vector $\mathbf{o}$ can be written as

$$||\mathbf{o}(\beta)||^2 = \sum_{k=1}^{2} \left(\sum_{j=1}^{h} (\tanh \beta y_j) \, v_{kj} \right)^2 \leq \sum_{j=1}^{h} (\tanh \beta y_j)^2 < \beta^2 \sum_{j=1}^{h} (\tanh y_j)^2 \ . \tag{C.18}$$

The last inequality follows from $\tanh(\beta)$ being a convex function for $\beta > 0$. Under the assumption $\tanh(y_j) = y_j$ and (C.16), the last term in (C.18) equals β^2. Thus,

$$||\mathbf{o}(\beta)|| < \beta \ . \tag{C.19}$$

Points further away from the circle are mapped closer to the circle (the training domain).

Appendix D

Database of hand-written digits

Figure D.1 shows the first images of each digit class from the MNIST database (LeCun, 1998). This database is freely available for download as a courtesy of Yann LeCun.

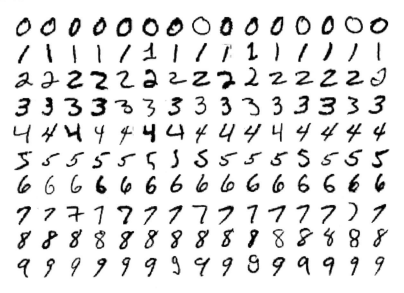

Figure D.1: The first digits from the MNIST database.

Appendix E

Notation and Symbols

Some mathematical notations are used throughout this book:

$\mathbf{x}$	a vector
$\mathbf{A}$	a matrix
x_i	component of the vector $\mathbf{x}$
a_{ij}	component of the matrix $\mathbf{A}$
$\mathbf{a}^T\mathbf{b}$	scalar product of the vectors $\mathbf{a}$ and $\mathbf{b}$
$\mathbf{ab}^T$	matrix with components $a_i b_j$ (direct product)
$\langle x \rangle$	expectation value of a random variable x
$\{\mathbf{x}_i\}$	set of vectors with index i
$p(\mathbf{x}\|j)$	probability of $\mathbf{x}$ given the condition j (conditional probability)

The meaning of often used symbols:

t	time (discrete)
S_t	sensory state at time t
M_t	motor command at time t
$\mathbb{R}$	set of all real numbers
n	number of training patterns
d	dimension of training patterns
m	number of units in a mixture, or for kernel PCA, the number of points in a reduced set
q	number of principal components
$\mathbf{c}_j$	code-book vector or the center of the unit j

169

C	covariance matrix of a data distribution
W	$d \times q$ matrix containing the principal components as columns
w	a principal component
λ^l	eigenvalue belonging to the principal component l
σ^2	residual variance per dimension. σ is also used as the width of a Gaussian function
K	kernel matrix

In this book, the following abbreviations appear:

PCA	principal component analysis (or analyzer)
MLP	multi-layer perceptron
RNN	recurrent neural network
SOM	self-organizing map
PSOM	parametrized self-organizing map
NGPCA	neural gas extended to principal component analysis
MPPCA	mixture of probabilistic principal component analyzers
RRLSA	robust recursive least square algorithm

Bibliography

Albrecht, S., Busch, J., Kloppenburg, M., Metze, F., and Tavan, P. (2000). Generalized radial basis function networks for classification and novelty detection: Self-organization of optimal bayesian decision. *Neural Networks*, **13**, 1075–1093.

Archambeau, C., Lee, J. A., and Verleysen, M. (2003). On convergence problems of the EM algorithm for finite gaussian mixtures. In Verleysen, M., (Ed.), *Proceedings of the European Symposium on Artificial Neural Networks (ESANN 2003)*, pages 99–106, Belgium. d-side.

Astafiev, S. V., Stanley, C. M., Shulman, G. L., and Corbetta, M. (2004). Extrastriate body area in human occipital cortex responds to the performance of motor actions. *Nature Neuroscience*, **7**, 542–548.

Bach-Y-Rita, P. (1972). *Brain Mechanisms in Sensory Substitution*. Academic Press, New York.

Bachmann, C. M., Cooper, L. N., Dembo, A., and Zeitouni, O. (1987). A relaxation model for memory with high storage density. *Proceedings of the National Academy of Sciences of the USA*, **84**, 7529–7531.

Baldi, P. and Heiligenberg, W. (1988). How sensory maps could enhance resolution through ordered arrangements of broadly tuned receivers. *Biological Cybernetics*, **59**, 313–318.

Batista, A. P., Buneo, C. A., Snyder, L. H., and Andersen, R. A. (1999). Reach plans in eye-centered coordinates. *Science*, **285**, 257–260.

Bishop, C. M. (1995). *Neural Networks for Pattern Recognition*. Oxford University Press, UK.

Blakemore, S. J., Wolpert, D., and Frith, C. (2000). Why can't you tickle yourself? *NeuroReport*, **11**, R11–R16.

Blanz, V. and Vetter, T. (1999). A morphable model for the synthesis of 3D faces. In Rockwood, A., (Ed.), *Siggraph 1999, Computer Graphics Proceedings*, pages 187–194, Los Angeles. Addison Wesley Longman.

Blasdel, G. G. and Salama, G. (1986). Voltage-sensitive dyes reveal a modular organization in monkey striate cortex. *Nature*, **321**, 579–585.

Brooks, R. A. (1986a). Achieving artificial intelligence through building robots. Technical Report A. I. Memo 899, Artificial Intelligence Laboratory, Massachusetts Institute of Technology, USA.

Brooks, R. A. (1986b). A robust layered control system for a mobile robot. *IEEE Journal of Robotics and Automation*, **RA-2**, 14–23.

Burges, C. J. C. (1996). Simplified support vector decision rules. In Saitta, L., (Ed.), *Proceedings of the 13th International Conference on Machine Learning*, pages 71–77, San Mateo, CA. Morgan Kaufmann.

Carter Jr., E. F. (1994). A general purpose simulated annealing class. http://www.taygeta.com/Classes.html.

Cipolla, R. and Hollinghurst, N. (1997). Visually guided grasping in unstructured environments. *Robotics and Autonomous Systems*, **19**, 337–346.

Colent, C., Pisella, L., Bernieri, C., Rode, G., and Rossetti, Y. (2000). Cognitive bias induced by visuo-motor adaptation to prisms: A simulation of unilateral neglect in normal individuals. *NeuroReport*, **11**, 1899–1902.

Cortes, C. and Vapnik, V. (1995). Support-vector networks. *Machine Learning*, **20**, 273–297.

Cover, T. M. (1965). Geometrical and statistical properties of systems of linear inequalities with applications in pattern recognition. *IEEE Transactions on Electronic Computers*, **14**, 326–334.

Cruse, H. (2001). Building robots with a complex motor system to understand cognition. In Webb, B. and Consi, T. R., (Eds.), *Biorobotics*, pages 107–120. MIT Press, Cambridge, MA.

Cruse, H. (2003a). The evolution of cognition—a hypothesis. *Cognitive Science*, **27**, 135–155.

Cruse, H. (2003b). A recurrent network for landmark-based navigation. *Biological Cybernetics*, **88**, 425–437.

Cruse, H. and Steinkühler, U. (1993). Solution of the direct and inverse kinematic problems by a common algorithm based on the mean of multiple computations. *Biological Cybernetics*, **69**, 345–351.

Daszykowski, M., Walczak, B., and Massart, D. L. (2002). On the optimal partitioning of data with k-means, growing k-means, neural gas, and growing neural gas. *Journal of Chemical Information and Computer Science*, **42**, 1378–1389.

Dembo, A. and Zeitouni, O. (1988). General potential surfaces and neural networks. *Physical Review A*, **37**, 2134–2143.

Dempster, A. P., Laird, N. M., and Rubin, D. B. (1977). Maximum likelihood from incomplete data via the EM algorithm. *Journal of the Royal Statistical Society. Series B*, **39**, 1–38.

Diamantaras, K. I. and Kung, S. Y. (1996). *Principal Component Neural Networks*. John Wiley & Sons, New York.

Distante, C., Anglani, A., and Taurisano, F. (2000). Target reaching by using visual information and Q-learning controllers. *Autonomous Robots*, **9**, 41–50.

Elman, J. L. (1990). Finding structure in time. *Cognitive Science*, **14**, 179–211.

Franz, V. H., Bülthoff, H. H., and Fahle, M. (2003). Grasp effects of the Ebbinghaus illusion: Obstacle avoidance is not the explanation. *Experimental Brain Research*, **149**, 470–477.

Fritzke, B. (1995). A growing neural gas network learns topologies. *Advances in Neural Information Processing Systems*, **7**, 625–632.

Fuentes, O. and Nelson, R. C. (1998). Learning dextrous manipulation skills for multifingered robot hands using the evolution strategy. *Machine Learning*, **31**, 223–237.

Gibson, J. J. (1977). The theory of affordances. In Shaw, R. and Bransford, J., (Eds.), *Perceiving, Acting, and Knowing*, chapter 3, pages 67–82. Erlbaum, Hillsdale, NJ.

Goodale, M. A. and Milner, A. D. (1992). Separate visual pathways for perception and action. *Trends in Neurosciences*, **15**, 20–25.

Gordon, I. E. (1989). *Theories of visual perception*. John Wiley & Sons, Chichester, UK.

Graziano, M. S., Taylor, C. S., and Moore, T. (2002). Complex movements evoked by microstimulation of precentral cortex. *Neuron*, **34**, 841–851.

Gregory, R. L. (1998). *Eye and Brain*, pages 136–169. Oxford University Press, UK.

Gregory, R. L. (2003). Seeing after blindness. *Nature Neuroscience*, **6**, 909–910.

Gross, H.-M., Heinze, A., Seiler, T., and Stephan, V. (1999). Generative character of perception: A neural architecture for sensorimotor anticipation. *Neural Networks*, **12**, 1101–1129.

Grush, R. (2004). The emulation theory of representation: Motor control, imagery, and perception. *Behavioral and Brain Sciences*, **27**, 377–442.

Harman, K. L., Humphrey, G. K., and Goodale, M. A. (1999). Active manual control of object views facilitates visual recognition. *Current Biology*, **9**, 1315–1318.

Hastie, T. and Stuetzle, W. (1989). Principal curves. *Journal of the American Statistical Association*, **84**, 502–516.

Haugeland, J. (1986). *Artificial Intelligence: The Very Idea*. MIT Press, Cambridge, MA.

Haykin, S. (1998). *Neural Networks: A Comprehensive Foundation*. Prentice Hall, Paramus, NJ.

Held, R. and Freedman, S. J. (1963). Plasticity in human sensorimotor control. *Science*, **142**, 455–462.

Held, R. and Hein, A. (1963). Movement-produced stimulation in the development of visually guided behaviour. *Journal of Comparative and Physiological Psychology*, **56**, 872–876.

Hertz, J., Krogh, A., and Palmer, R. G. (1991). *Introduction to the Theory of Neural Computation*. Addison-Wesley, Redwood City, CA.

Hesslow, G. (2002). Conscious thought as simulation of behaviour and perception. *Trends in Cognitive Sciences*, **6**, 242–247.

Hinton, G. E., Dayan, P., and Revow, M. (1997). Modeling the manifolds of images of handwritten digits. *IEEE Transactions on Neural Networks*, **8**, 65–74.

Hoffmann, H. and Möller, R. (2003). Unsupervised learning of a kinematic arm model. In Kaynak, O., Alpaydin, E., Oja, E., and Xu, L., (Eds.), *Artificial Neural Networks and Neural Information Processing—ICANN/ICONIP 2003, LNCS*, volume 2714, pages 463–470. Springer, Berlin.

Hoffmann, H. and Möller, R. (2004). Action selection and mental transformation based on a chain of forward models. In Schaal, S., Ijspeert, A., Billard, A., Vijayakumar, S., Hallam, J., and Meyer, J.-A., (Eds.), *From Animals to Animats 8, Proceedings of the Eighth International Conference on the Simulation of Adaptive Behavior*, pages 213–222, Los Angeles, CA. MIT Press.

Hopfield, J. J. (1982). Neural networks and physical systems with emergent collective computational abilities. *Proceedings of the National Academy of Sciences of the USA*, **79**, 2554–2558.

Hopfield, J. J. (1984). Neurons with graded response have collective computational properties like those of two-state neurons. *Proceedings of the National Academy of Sciences of the USA*, **81**, 3088–3092.

Hubel, D. H. and Wiesel, T. N. (1962). Receptive fields, binocular interaction and functional architecture in the cat's visual cortex. *Journal of Physiology*, **160**, 106–154.

James, K. H., Humphrey, G. K., Vilis, T., Corrie, B., Baddour, R., and Goodale, M. A. (2002). "Active" and "passive" learning of three-dimensional object structure within an immersive virtual reality environment. *Behavior Research Methods, Instruments, and Computers*, **34**, 383–390.

Jeannerod, M. (2001). Neural simulation of action: A unifying mechanism for motor cognition. *NeuroImage*, **14**, S103–S109.

Jirenhed, D.-A., Hesslow, G., and Ziemke, T. (2001). Exploring internal simulation of perception in mobile robots. *Lund University Cognitive Studies*, **86**, 107–113.

Jordan, M. I. and Rumelhart, D. E. (1992). Forward models: Supervised learning with a distal teacher. *Cognitive Science*, **16**, 307–354.

Kambhatla, N. and Leen, T. K. (1997). Dimension reduction by local principal component analysis. *Neural Computation*, **9**, 1493–1516.

Kawato, M., Furukawa, K., and Suzuki, R. (1987). A hierarchical neural-network model for control and learning of voluntary movement. *Biological Cybernetics*, **57**, 169–185.

Kohonen, T. (1982). Self-organized formation of topologically correct feature maps. *Biological Cybernetics*, **43**, 59–69.

Kohonen, T. (1989). *Self-Organization and Associative Memory, 3rd edition*. Springer, Berlin.

Kohonen, T. (1995). *Self-Organizing Maps*. Springer, Berlin.

Kuperstein, M. (1988). Neural model of adaptive hand-eye coordination for single postures. *Science*, **239**, 1308–1311.

Kuperstein, M. (1990). INFANT neural controller for adaptive sensory-motor coordination. *Neural Networks*, **4**, 131–145.

Latham, P. E., Deneve, S., and Pouget, A. (2003). Optimal computation with attractor networks. *Journal of Physiology*, **97**, 683–694.

LeCun, Y. (1998). The MNIST database of handwritten digits. NEC Research Institute, http://yann.lecun.com/exdb/mnist/index.html.

LeCun, Y., Bottou, L., Bengio, Y., and Haffner, P. (1998). Gradient-based learning applied to document recognition. *Proceedings of the IEEE*, **86**, 2278–2324.

Linde, Y., Buzo, A., and Gray, R. M. (1980). An algorithm for vector quantizer design. *IEEE Transactions on Communications*, **28**, 84–95.

Linden, D. E. J., Kallenbach, U., Heinecke, A., Singer, W., and Goebel, R. (1999). The myth of upright vision. A psychophysical and functional imaging study of adaptation to inverting spectacles. *Perception*, **28**, 469–481.

Lloyd, S. P. (1982). Least squares quantization in PCM. *IEEE Transactions on Information Theory*, **28**, 129–137.

Luria, S. M. and Kinney, J. A. S. (1970). Underwater vision. *Science*, **167**, 1454–1461.

Mallot, H. A., Kopecz, J., and von Seelen, W. (1992). Neuroinformatik als empirische Wissenschaft. *Kognitionswissenschaft*, **3**, 12–13.

Martinetz, T. M., Berkovich, S. G., and Schulten, K. J. (1993). "Neural-Gas" network for vector quantization and its application to time-series prediction. *IEEE Transactions on Neural Networks*, **4**, 558–569.

Martinetz, T. M. and Schulten, K. J. (1990). Hierarchical neural net for learning control of a robot's arm and gripper. In *Proceedings of the International Joint Conference on Neural Networks*, volume 3, pages 747–752. IEEE, New York.

Meinicke, P. (2000). *Unsupervised Learning in a Generalized Regression Framework*. PhD thesis, Faculty of Technology, Bielefeld University, Germany.

Meinicke, P. and Ritter, H. (2001). Resolution-based complexity control for gaussian mixture models. *Neural Computation*, **13**, 453–475.

Micchelli, C. A. (1986). Interpolation of scattered data: Distance matrices and conditionally positive definite functions. *Constructive Approximation*, **2**, 11–22.

Mika, S., Schölkopf, B., Smola, A. J., Müller, K.-R., Scholz, M., and Rätsch, G. (1999). Kernel PCA and de-noising in feature spaces. *Advances in Neural Information Processing Systems*, **11**, 536–542.

Miller, J. P., Jacobs, G. A., and Theunissen, F. E. (1991). Representation of sensory information in the cricket cercal sensory system. I. Response properties of the primary interneurons. *Journal of Neurophysiology*, **66**, 1680–1689.

Molina-Vilaplana, J., Pedreño-Molina, J. L., and López-Coronado, J. (2004). Hyper RBF model for accurate reaching in redundant robotic systems. *Neurocomputing*, **61**, 495–501.

Möller, R. (1996). *Wahrnehmung durch Vorhersage—Eine Konzeption der handlungsorientierten Wahrnehmung*. PhD thesis, Faculty of Computer Science and Automation, Ilmenau Technical University, Germany.

Möller, R. (1999). Perception through anticipation—a behavior-based approach to visual perception. In Riegler, A., Peschl, M., and von Stein, A., (Eds.), *Understanding Representation in the Cognitive Sciences*, pages 169–176. Plenum Academic / Kluwer Publishers, New York.

Möller, R. (2002). Interlocking of learning and orthonormalization in RRLSA. *Neurocomputing*, **49**, 429–433.

Möller, R. and Hoffmann, H. (2004). An extension of neural gas to local PCA. *Neurocomputing*, **62**, 305–326.

Moody, J. and Darken, C. J. (1989). Fast learning in networks of locally-tuned processing units. *Neural Computation*, **1**, 281–294.

Movellan, J. R. and McClelland, J. L. (1993). Learning continuous probability distributions with symmetric diffusion networks. *Cognitive Science*, **17**, 463–496.

Murata, A., Fadiga, L., Fogassi, L., Gallese, V., Raos, V., and Rizzolatti, G. (1997). Object representation in the ventral premotor cortex (area F5) of the monkey. *Journal of Neurophysiology*, **78**, 2226–2230.

Nakazawa, K., Quirk, M. C., Chitwood, R. A., Watanabe, M., Yeckel, M. F., Sun, L. D., Kato, A., Carr, C. A., Johnston, D., Wilson, M. A., and Tonegawa, S. (2002). Requirement for hippocampal CA3 NMDA receptors in associative memory recall. *Science*, **297**, 211–218.

Oja, E. (1982). A simplified neuron model as a principal component analyzer. *Journal of Mathematical Biology*, **15**, 267–273.

Oja, E. (1989). Neural networks, principle components, and subspaces. *International Journal of Neural Systems*, **1**, 61–68.

O'Regan, J. K. and Noë, A. (2001). A sensorimotor account of vision and visual consciousness. *Behavioral and Brain Sciences*, **24**, 939–1031.

Ouyang, S., Bao, Z., and Liao, G.-S. (2000). Robust recursive least squares learning algorithm for principal component analysis. *IEEE Transactions on Neural Networks*, **11**, 215–221.

Oztop, E., Bradley, N. S., and Arbib, M. A. (2004). Infant grasp learning: A computational model. *Experimental Brain Research*, **158**, 480–503.

Parzen, E. (1962). On estimation of a probability density function and mode. *Annals of Mathematical Statistics*, **33**, 1065–1076.

Pelah, A. and Barlow, H. B. (1996). Visual illusion from running. *Nature*, **381**, 283–283.

Pfeifer, R. and Scheier, C. (1999). *Understanding Intelligence*. MIT Press, Cambridge, MA.

Philipona, D., O'Regan, J. K., and Nadal, J.-P. (2003). Is there something out there? Inferring space from sensorimotor dependencies. *Neural Computation*, **15**, 2029–2049.

Philipona, D., O'Regan, J. K., Nadal, J.-P., and Coenen, O. J.-M. D. (2004). Perception of the structure of the physical world using unknown multimodal sensors and effectors. In *Advances in Neural Information Processing Systems*, volume 16. MIT Press.

Pouget, A., Dayan, P., and Zemel, R. S. (2003). Inference and computation with population codes. *Annual Review of Neuroscience*, **26**, 381–410.

Press, W. H., Teukolsky, S. A., Vetterling, W. T., and Flannery, B. P. (1993). *Numerical Recipes in C: The Art of Scientific Computing*. Cambridge University Press, UK.

Prinz, W. (1997). Perception and action planning. *European Journal of Cognitive Psychology*, **9**, 129–154.

Qiu, G., Varley, M. R., and Terrell, T. J. (1994). Improved clustering using deterministic annealing with a gradient descent technique. *Pattern Recognition Letters*, **15**, 607–610.

Riedmiller, M. and Braun, H. (1993). A direct adaptive method for faster backpropagation learning: The RPROP algorithm. In *Proceedings of the IEEE International Conference on Neural Networks*, pages 586–591, San Francisco, CA.

Ritter, H., Martinetz, T., and Schulten, K. (1990). *Neuronale Netze*. Addison-Wesley, Bonn, Germany.

Ritter, H. J. (1993). Parametrized self-organizing maps. In Gielen, S. and Kappen, B., (Eds.), *Proceedings of the International Conference on Artificial Neural Networks*, pages 568–575. Springer, Berlin.

Ritter, H. J., Martinetz, T. M., and Schulten, K. J. (1989). Topology-conserving maps for learning visuo-motor-coordination. *Neural Networks*, **2**, 159–168.

Ritter, H. J. and Schulten, K. J. (1986). Topology conserving mappings for learning motor tasks. In Denker, J. S., (Ed.), *Neural Networks for Computing*, volume 151, pages 376–380, Snowbird, UT. AIP Conference Proceedings.

Rizzolatti, G., Camarda, R., Fogassi, L., Gentilucci, M., Luppino, G., and Matelli, M. (1988). Functional organization of inferior area 6 in the macaque monkey. *Experimental Brain Research*, **71**, 491–507.

Rizzolatti, G. and Fadiga, L. (1998). Grasping objects and grasping action meanings: The dual role of monkey rostroventral premotor cortex (area F5). *Novartis Foundation Symposium*, **218**, 81–103.

Rizzolatti, G., Fogassi, L., and Gallese, V. (2001). Neurophysiological mechanisms underlying the understanding and imitation of action. *Nature Reviews Neuroscience*, **2**, 661–670.

Rose, K. (1998). Deterministic annealing for clustering, compression, classification, regression, and related optimization problems. *Proceedings of the IEEE*, **86**, 2210–2239.

Rose, K., Gurewitz, E., and Fox, G. C. (1990). Statistical mechanics and phase transitions in clustering. *Physical Review Letters*, **65**, 945–948.

Rossetti, Y., Rode, G., Pisella, L., Farné, A., Li, L., Boisson, D., and Perenin, M.-T. (1998). Prism adaptation to a rightward optical deviation rehabilitates left hemispatial neglect. *Nature*, **395**, 166–169.

Rubner, J. and Tavan, P. (1989). A self-organizing network for principal-component analysis. *Europhysics Letters*, **10**, 693–698.

Salganicoff, M., Ungar, L. H., and Bajcsy, R. (1996). Active learning for vision-based robot grasping. *Machine Learning*, **23**, 251–278.

Sanger, T. D. (1989). Optimal unsupervised learning in a single-layer linear feedforward neural network. *Neural Networks*, **2**, 459–473.

Schenck, W., Hoffmann, H., and Möller, R. (2003). Learning internal models for eye-hand coordination in reaching and grasping. In *Proceedings of the European Cognitive Science Conference*, pages 289–294. Erlbaum, Mahwah, NJ.

Schenck, W. and Möller, R. (2004). Staged learning of saccadic eye movements with a robot camera head. In Bowman, H. and Labiouse, C., (Eds.), *Connectionist Models of Cognition and Perception II*, pages 82–91. World Scientific, London, NJ.

Schölkopf, B., Knirsch, P., Smola, A. J., and Burges, C. (1998a). Fast approximation of support vector kernel expansions, and an interpretation of clustering as approximation in feature spaces. In Levi, P., Ahlers, R.-J., May, F., and Schanz, M., (Eds.), *20. DAGM Symposium Mustererkennung*, pages 124–132. Springer, Berlin.

Schölkopf, B. and Smola, A. J. (2002). *Learning with Kernels*. MIT Press, Cambridge, MA.

Schölkopf, B., Smola, A. J., and Müller, K.-R. (1998b). Nonlinear component analysis as a kernel eigenvalue problem. *Neural Computation*, **10**, 1299–1319.

Simons, D. J. and Wang, R. F. (1998). Perceiving real-world viewpoint changes. *Psychological Science*, **9**, 315–320.

Simpson, J. and Weiner, E., (Eds.) (1989). *Oxford English Dictionary, Second Edition*. Oxford University Press, UK.

Steinkühler, U. and Cruse, H. (1998). A holistic model for an internal representation to control the movement of a manipulator with redundant degrees of freedom. *Biological Cybernetics*, **79**, 457–466.

Stratton, G. M. (1896). Some preliminary experiments on vision without inversion of the retinal image. *Psychological Review*, **3**, 611–617.

Stratton, G. M. (1897). Vision without inversion of the retinal image. *Psychological Review*, **4**, 341–360; 463–481.

Sugita, Y. (1996). Global plasticity in adult visual cortex following reversal of visual input. *Nature*, **380**, 523–526.

Sun, H.-J., Campos, J. L., and Chan, G. S. W. (2003). Multisensory integration in the estimation of relative path length. *Experimental Brain Research*, **154**, 246–254.

Szu, H. and Hartley, R. (1987). Fast simulated annealing. *Physics Letters A*, **122**, 157–162.

Tani, J. (1996). Model-based learning for mobile robot navigation from the dynamical systems perspective. *IEEE Transactions on Systems, Man, and Cybernetics—Part B*, **26**, 421–436.

Tani, J. and Nolfi, S. (1999). Learning to perceive the world as articulated: An approach for hierarchical learning in sensory-motor systems. *Neural Networks*, **12**, 1131–1141.

Tavan, P., Grubmüller, H., and Kühnel, H. (1990). Self-organization of associative memory and pattern classification: Recurrent signal processing on topological feature maps. *Biological Cybernetics*, **64**, 95–105.

Tipping, M. E. and Bishop, C. M. (1997). Probabilistic principal component analysis. Technical Report 010, Neural Computing Research Group.

Tipping, M. E. and Bishop, C. M. (1999). Mixtures of probabilistic principal component analyzers. *Neural Computation*, **11**, 443–482.

Tolman, E. C. (1932). *Purposive Behavior in Animals and Men*. The Century Co., New York.

Treue, S. and Trujillo, J. C. M. (1999). Feature-based attention influences motion processing gain in macaque visual cortex. *Nature*, **399**, 575–579.

Uno, Y., Fukumura, N., Suzuki, R., and Kawato, M. (1995). A computational model for recognizing objects and planning hand shapes in grasping movements. *Neural Networks*, **8**, 839–851.

Walter, J. A., Nölker, C., and Ritter, H. (2000). The PSOM algorithm and applications. In *Proceedings of the Symposium on Neural Computation*, pages 758–764.

Webb, B. (2001). Can robots make good models of biological behaviour? *Behavioral and Brain Sciences*, **24**, 1033–1050.

Wentzell, A. (2003). Tulane University, Math 301, Lecture 19, Problem 6.

Wexler, M. and Klam, F. (2001). Movement prediction and movement production. *Journal of Experimental Psychology: Human Perception and Performance*, **27**, 48–64.

Wohlschläger, A. (2001). Mental object rotation and the planning of hand movements. *Perception & Psychophysics*, **63**, 709–718.

Wolpert, D. M., Ghahramani, Z., and Jordan, M. I. (1995). An internal model for sensorimotor integration. *Science*, **269**, 1880–1882.

Yair, E., Zeger, K., and Gersho, A. (1992). Competitive learning and soft competition for vector quantizer design. *IEEE Transactions on Signal Processing*, **40**, 294–309.